Science and Democracy

Laura Pantzerhielm

The FORSCHUNGSBERICHTE INTERNATIONALE POLITIK are presenting the research results of members and fellows from the *Center for Transnational Relations, Foreign and Security Policy* of the Otto-Suhr-Institute for Political Science at the Department of Political and Social Sciences, Freie Universität Berlin. The reports focus on the foreign and security policies of Germany and the United States of America as well as the larger themes of transatlantic relations and European security. Analysis is based upon a broad understanding of 'security', which encompasses traditional military and defence policy issues as well as new security risks. Various dimensions of international relations relevant to security and governance issues on the state, transnational or international level, such as questions of human rights, economics, culture and identity, are addressed.

Editor's address:

Ingo Peters
Freie Universität Berlin,
Department of Political and Social Sciences
Center for Transnational Relations,
Foreign and Security Policy
Ihnestr. 22, 14195 Berlin,
Phone +49 (0)30 / 838-55530
ingo@zedat.fu-berlin.de

FORSCHUNGSBERICHTE
INTERNATIONALE POLITIK

45

Science and Democracy

Contingent regularities in scholarly discourse on European governance

Laura Pantzerhielm

LIT VERLAG

Bibliographic information published by the Deutsche Nationalbibliothek
The Deutsche Nationalbibliothek lists this publication in the Deutsche Nationalbibliografie; detailed bibliographic data are available on the Internet at http://dnb.d-nb.de.

ISBN 978-3-643-90724-0

A catalogue record for this book is available from the British Library

Zweigniederlassung Zürich 2016
Klosbachstr. 107
CH-8032 Zürich
Tel. +41 (0) 44-251 75 05 Fax +41 (0) 44-251 75 06
E-Mail: zuerich@lit-verlag.ch http://www.lit-verlag.ch

Distribution:

In the UK: Global Book Marketing, e-mail: mo@centralbooks.com
In North America: International Specialized Book Services, e-mail: orders@isbs.com
In Germany: LIT Verlag Fresnostr. 2, D-48159 Münster
Tel. +49 (0) 2 51-620 32 22, Fax +49 (0) 2 51-922 60 99, E-mail: vertrieb@lit-verlag.de

In Austria: Medienlogistik Pichler-ÖBZ, e-mail: mlo@medien-logistik.at
e-books are available at www.litwebshop.de

FORSCHUNGSBERICHTE
INTERNATIONALE POLITIK

45

Science and Democracy

Contingent regularities in scholarly discourse on European governance

Laura Pantzerhielm

LIT VERLAG

Bibliographic information published by the Deutsche Nationalbibliothek
The Deutsche Nationalbibliothek lists this publication in the Deutsche Nationalbibliografie; detailed bibliographic data are available on the Internet at http://dnb.d-nb.de.

ISBN 978-3-643-90724-0

A catalogue record for this book is available from the British Library

Klosbachstr. 107
CH-8032 Zürich
Tel. +41 (0) 44-251 75 05 Fax +41 (0) 44-251 75 06
E-Mail: zuerich@lit-verlag.ch http://www.lit-verlag.ch

Distribution:

In the UK: Global Book Marketing, e-mail: mo@centralbooks.com
In North America: International Specialized Book Services, e-mail: orders@isbs.com
In Germany: LIT Verlag Fresnostr. 2, D-48159 Münster
Tel. +49 (0) 2 51-620 32 22, Fax +49 (0) 2 51-922 60 99, E-mail: vertrieb@lit-verlag.de
In Austria: Medienlogistik Pichler-ÖBZ, e-mail: mlo@medien-logistik.at
e-books are available at www.litwebshop.de

Acknowledgements

The present study came about as a master's thesis in Political Science at Freie Universität Berlin in the summer term of 2014. I am very much indebted to my first supervisor Prof. Dr. Brigitte Kerchner for placing her trust in the project despite its slightly venturesome nature, for her insightful advice on the theoretical background and methodological implications of Foucauldian discourse analysis as well as for her personal encouragement and support throughout the research process. I would also like to express my sincere gratitude to my second supervisor Prof. Dr. Anna Holzscheiter for her constructive and precise feedback, for pointing me to further relevant strands of literature and sharing her expertise on the nexus of discourse analysis and International Relations research. I would like to thank my friend and editor Max Bach for doing an excellent job in editing and correcting the manuscript.

I am grateful to the Berlin Social Science Center (WZB) for providing financial support for this publication. In particular, I would like to thank Jan-Hinrich Wagner and Babette Hagemann for their kind assistance.

Last but not least, I would like to extend my warm thanks to Dr. Ingo Peters, the editor of the present series "Forschungsberichte internationale Politik", as well as to Veit D. Hopf from LIT-Verlag for making this publication possible.

Table of Contents

Abbreviations

CSDP	Common Security and Defence Policy
JCMS	Journal of Common Market Studies
EfD	European Endowment for Democracy
EIDHR	European Instrument for Democracy and Human Rights
ENP	European Neighbourhood Policy
EP	European Parliament
EU	European Union MS Member State
OSCE	Organization for Security and Cooperation in Europe
TEU	Treaty of the European Union

1 Introduction

"La 'démocratie représentative' peut sembler aujourd'hui un pléonasme. Mais cela a d'abord été un oxymore." (Jacques Rancière 2005)

1.1 Perceptions of Democracy in Discourses on EU Governance

Alongside human rights, peace and the rule of law, the success and spread of democracy forms an ever reoccurring element in contemporary narratives and stories circulating about the European Union (EU) and the role it plays in the world. Within both the institutional discourse of the Union itself and pertinent strands of social science literature, "democracy" is often perceived as belonging to a stable set of European norms and values which the Union is seeking to export to external territories (cf. *inter alia* Manner 2002, Rogers 2007, Börzel/Risse 2009; European Council 2002, European Commission 2011a, 2011b, Van Rompuy/Barroso 2012). For instance, the joint statement presented by Herman Van Rompuy and José Manuel Barroso as the EU was awarded with the Nobel Peace Prize in 2012, neatly summarized this ubiquitous tale about a "reunified" European continent built "around values of respect for human dignity, freedom, democracy, equality, the rule of law and respect for human rights," which engages in advancing its values elsewhere "in order to make the world a better place for all" (Van Rompuy/Barroso 2012). Underlying contemporary discourses on the EU and its external relations, one can thus discern a perception that governing techniques directed towards other regions derive from and strengthen European values, with democracy inhabiting a central position. Besides resulting perceptions of general external-relations instruments such as the European Neighbourhood Policy (ENP), the Common Security and Defence Policy (CSDP), bilateral trade agreements and development aid as reflecting an European quality of democracy and an associated concern with its universalization, an increasing number of targeted "democracy promotion" programs have been established in recent years, with the stated purpose to promote "the European values of freedom and democracy" (EfD 2014, cf. Burnell 2000, Risse/Börzel 2004, 2009).

So far, a majority of IR and European integration research has approached these discourses and the general nexus of EU/European governance, external relations and democracy in two ways. Research strands concerned with questions about the nature of the EU's external relations often tend to echo the institutional discourse by placing "European values", "norms" and/or "principles" in a continuum with the EU's foreign-policy identity and by describing the influence that the Union exerts in the international realm as a "soft", "ethical" or "normative" kind of power (Manners 2002, Manners 2006, Börzel/Risse 2009, Anderson /Seitz 2006, Grevi/Helly/Keohane 2009). Research on "democracy promotion" programs has instead been primarily concerned with isolating causal relations, inter-case variation in level of success and the practical feasibility of programs carried out by the EU and other international actors to build, strengthen, promote or assist democratization (*inter alia* Burnell 2000, Barany/Moser 2009, Börzel/Risse 2009, Cox/Ikenberry/ Inoguchi 2000, Craner/Wollack 2008, Diamond 2008, Laxenex/Schimmelfennig 2009, 2011, Piccone/Youngs 2006, Schimmelfennig/Scholtz 2008, Youngs 2002, 2008, 2009).

The present thesis proposes an alternative starting point for understanding contemporary discourses that establish "democracy" as an object of EU/European governance. Rather than looking at technical efficiency ("success" of programs), or norm diffusion and compliance (spread of democratic governance), I believe a focus on discourse in the sense of overarching "representational scripts" (Holzscheiter 2013: 18) and a historical-genealogical perspective asking how such scripts emerged over time and attained their contemporary sense of naturalness to be particularly useful in throwing light on contemporary perceptions and practices. More specifically, I investigate contemporary discourses by applying a Foucauldian perspective that pays attention to discursive instability and historical specificity/contingence, while putting an analytical focus on regularities in text and speech. Such a perspective opens up a systematic consideration of what constitutes "democracy" as an object in the context of EU/European governance, asking how the perception of democracy as an EU/European value and foreign-policy goal is stabilized by other discursive regularities and also for subverting their contemporary sense of naturalness. Before discussing the main theoretical concepts and specifying the methodological implications of such a perspective (2.1-2.3), I would like to briefly discuss some further motives for choosing this particular approach.

On a theoretical level, if one conceives of discursive objects such as the term "democracy" as historically contingent, productive representations of the social world which are continuously reproduced in text and speech, the way in which meaning is fixed and transformed gains analytical importance. Moreover, if one deduces from the claim that discursive articulations are contingent that any given discursive articulation entails exclusion of other possibilities, the power effects of dominant representations, including scientific knowledge and truths, merit systematic attention. In short: the excluding nature of representation indicates its inherent contingency and instability, thus pointing to discursive fixation of meaning, knowledge and ensuing power effects as promising analytical categories. In IR, the resulting perspective on knowledge, language and power as inextricably intertwined has been drawn upon by scholars like Thomas Diez, David Campbell, James Derian and Michel Shapiro, who are usually categorized as "post-structuralists" when maps and overviews of the discipline's landscape are drawn (cf. Diez 2007: 471; Campbell 1999, 2007: 204-5, Der Derian/Shapiro 1989, Foucault [1970] 2010). However, this view of power and knowledge is also shared by a number of theorists who place themselves in a Marxist tradition while arguing for an anti-essentialist and post-positivist epistemological perspective, including, for instance, Chantal Mouffe and Ernesto Laclau, Claude Lefort or Jacques Rancières.[1]

Such a focus on discourse, knowledge, mechanisms of exclusion and power effects seems particularly relevant when analyzing articulations surrounding and constituting the term "democracy" given the multiplicity of conceptual historical transformations and the wide range of interpretations within both political philosophy, practical discourses on government and social struggles that it has been subject to. This observation supports Milja Kurki's call for tackling "the *conceptual underpinnings* of

---

1 Put in general terms, the latter have drawn on Foucault, Jacques Derrida and others to question and deconstruct the divisions between bourgeois ideology and true scientific (Marxist) knowledge, but also between material base and ideational superstructure, which are inherent to orthodox, classical Marxism and instead propagate an anti-essentialist epistemological position and a post-positivist view of knowledge (Mouffe/Laclau [1985] 2001 105-7, Mouffe 2007: 27, Lefort 1990: 285, 2012, Rancière 1979, 2002, on anti-essentialism and the concept of discourse in Mouffe and Laclau cf. also Marchart 2007: 107).

democratization and democracy promotion" rather than limiting scholarly inquiry to collecting data on individual cases of intervention (Kurki 2010: v). Kurki also joins with other IR scholars in making an empirical argument for taking discursive instability seriously when studying contemporary perceptions and practices drawing on terms like "democracy" and "democratization" by pointing to the increased contestation, skepticism and resistance towards democracy promotion programs that has emerged in "target countries" since the late 2000s (Kurki 2010: iv, Wolff 2013, Burron 2012).

Finally, from my point of view, the combination of conceptual vagueness, the strong normative connotation that the term "democracy" has been endowed with since the early 1990s, the parallel emergence of new governing techniques that draw heavily on the concept and its central position in dominant contemporary EU narratives makes studying discourses proliferating around it worthwhile. To put it plainly: it is hard to be against democracy, but at the same time it is also hard to define it. Thus, the prerogative of interpretation over the term and knowledge production about what it entails is intimately connected with power.

Against the backdrop of these considerations, the present thesis therefore asks and seeks to investigate the following central research question:

- How can contemporary discourses constituting "democracy" as an object of speech in the context of EU/European governance be described in terms of their regularities, exclusions and borders of what is (reasonably) speakable?

In the following chapters, I first outline the state of research on the various connections between EU governance, external relations and democracy in more detail, while paying special attention to critical and discourse-theoretical approaches (1.2). Thereafter, I turn to the central theoretical concepts and implications of Foucauldian discourse analysis (2.2), seek to clarify what distinguishes it from other approaches to discourse in political science and IR (2.1), discuss how it can be implemented as a research methodology and delimit two text corpuses (2.3) that serve as a basis for the ensuing primary analysis (3- 4).

1.2 The State of Research

The current state of research at the nexus of democracy, the EU and international politics can be divided into different categories. To start with, the term "democracy" figures prominently in generic research stran-ds on EU external relations. As I touched upon above, in this context, "democracy" is often perceived to belong to a list of values that, while deriving from history and culture, characterize the present EU and in particular its foreign policy identity as a "civilian" (Duchêne 1972) or "normative power" (Manners 2002). Within this research agenda, EU external relations governance is often described as a value-driven, less coercive kind of foreign policy-making that distinguishes itself from the self-interest and violent methods employed by other international actors and/or during previous eras in international politics (Diez/Manners 2007). For instance, social constructivist IR literature on the EU as a "normative power" depicts the Union as a novel kind of foreign-policy actor that is driven by a concern about universalizing (European) norms rather than by material interests. Empirical investigations drawing on the normative power concept thus focus on norm diffusion and compliance, rather than on (re)production or contingency, by exploring the extent to which the Union has been – and causal conditions for it to be – successful in exporting "its" norms and values (Manners 2002, Manners 2006, Börzel/Risse 2009, Anderson/Seitz 2006, Grevi/Helly/Keohane 2009).

IR post-structuralists have argued for viewing this scholarly debate as a site of discursive identity construction, where oppositions are established and reproduced that stabilize perceptions of an EU/European Self as distinguishable from a non-European Other or Outside (see, Thomas Diez's position in Diez/Manners 2007). Rather than analyzing the discursive constitution and emergence of alleged European values as such (human rights, rule of law, democracy, peace, prosperity etc.), this literature has hence focused on othering practices in contemporary EU external relations text, speech and academic (IR) literature that turn "third parties into 'others' and [represent] the EU as a positive force in world politics" (Diez 2005: 613).

As mentioned earlier, mainstream or objectivist strands of European studies and IR scholarship including social/moderate constructivist approaches have also produced a broad literature seeking to define causal mechanisms that determine the dynamics of externally induced or assisted democratization processes and related foreign policy governance techniques. For instance, Schimmelfennig and Scholz' study of 36 countries in the EU neighborhood concludes that there are "robust and strong effects of EU political conditionality on democracy" (2008: 187), while Ryan Kennedy's empirical investigation purports to indicate posit-ive causal effects of supranational identities on the prospects of success for democratization processes and the spread of "democratic values" (Kennedy 2013). Further studies operating from similarly objectivist epistemological standpoints are concerned with the "effectiveness" of external relations policy programs, a concept that is often understood in terms of an (economic) input - (transformational political) output relationship: "Is Europe spending enough on democracy assistance, and spending it in the best ways?" (Youngs 2008: 160, cf. also Burnell 2007).

Beyond questions about causalities, success and effectiveness, foreign policy discourse and governance practices drawing on notions such as "democracy promotion" or "democratization" have also been analyzed from critical and post-structuralist perspectives. Despite employing different theoretical-methodological approaches and using different empirical material, a number of such analyses make similar observations about the prominence of economic knowledge and rationalities in such articulations. Kurki (2011) draws on Foucault's *Birth of Biopolitics* ([1979] 2008) to investigate the European Instrument for Democracy and Human Rights (EIDHR) – the instrument employed by the EU to promote democratization in third countries through financial support to civil-society organizations. The instrument, she argues, can be understood as an expression of neoliberal governmentality foregrounding "liberal economic rationalities and interventions as essential in fostering free and prosperous societies" (Kurki 2011: 362). According to Kurki, the EIDHR ultimately seeks to extend economic free-market rationality, to foster entrepreneurial, free and active subjects and to direct power away from the state towards a self-regulating civil society (Kurki 2011: 362-3, 366-8).

Nicolas Guilhot (2005) draws similar conclusions, albeit from a Bourdieuian perspective. He identifies external democracy promotion as a part of a neoliberal orthodoxy, which, starting in the 1980s, incorpor-ated "progressive rhetoric" on democracy and human rights into an agenda for advancing free-market and entrepreneurial economic governance on a global scale (Guilhot 2005). Finally, neo-Gramscian scholars also point to the presence of "neoliberal" economic rationalities when analyzing US external democracy-promotion governing techniques (Robinson 2013, Burron 2011, 2012). Here, the term "neoliberal" is not so much associated with subjectivation or power relations in the Foucauldian sense, but with discursive naturalization of market processes in the sense of "a political code that restricts democratic control over the economy and sanctifies the logic of the market" (Burron 2012: 1658, cf. also 2011). This strand of critical scholarship also underlines the historical specificity of what they identify as the contemporary hegemonic discursive articulation, where "democracy" is equated with political representation, general elections and party pluralism. Following Robinson, such an understanding of what "democracy" entails effectively amounts to a stabilization of polyarchic (capitalist) rule (cf. Burron 2012, Robinson 2013: 230). Regardless of the differences in their respective theoretical approach and empirical material, Burron, Robinson, Guilhot and Kurki all point to the presence of perceptions and strategies stemming from knowledge production in the economic field in discourses constituting "external democracy promotion" and "democratization". Together with Robinson and Burron's observation of a discursive constitution of democracy as a combination of political representation, general elections and party pluralism that is seen as compatible with *de facto* elite rule, these findings are thus relevant to the leading question of the present investigation.

While claims about the "historical contingency" of contemporary perceptions in and of international politics are at the center of post-structuralist and critical IR research (cf. Diez 2007, Campbell 2007), few analyses draw on historical material when analyzing EU democracy promotion or the perception of democracy as an EU/European value or norm. However, Christopher Hobson's call for a "radical historicization" of democracy as a concept in IR research provides for a notable exception in this regard (2009). Hobson identifies narratives about liberal democracy as a universal, normatively superior form of government that progressively spreads around the globe as a consequence of historical progress as the dominant contemporary perception in both international affairs and IR research (2009: 634-7). In order to illustrate the fragility of such narratives, he then sets out to outline the distinctiveness of liberalism and democracy as historical intellectual traditions "respectively concerned with liberty and equality" (2009: 339), thus illustrating the relative novelty and nonnecessity of the "unlikely marriage" of the two concepts in Europe and the United States in the 20th century (2009: 633, 639-40.)

To sum up, the current state of research at the nexus of EU governance, external relations and democracy amounts to a rather fragmented picture. On the one hand, the central currents of mainstream research range from attempts to define causalities, measure the success and effectiveness of democratization and democracy promotion governance techniques, to constructivist analyses engaging in descriptions of the EU as a "normative power" and attempt to define causal factors explaining the diffusion of and compliance with "European" norms and values. Critical and post-structuralist approaches on the other hand have re-conceptualized the normative power debate as an othering practice in EU external relations and sought to uncover the historical non-necessity of contemporarily taken for granted discursive connections between democracy and liberalism. Moreover, critical and post-structuralist scholars have also engaged in analyses of what is understood to be an incorporation of neoliberal, free market rationalities and entrepreneurial, activating subjectivations into practices and discourses forming around concepts such as "external democracy promotion" and "democratization".

2 Theoretical and Methodological Approach

2.1 What's in a Word? Discourse in Political Science and IR

How does a Foucauldian approach position itself in this context and what does the use of Foucauldian discourse analysis imply? Both political science and IR research have seen an increasing interest in how perceptions of reality are (re)produced through language and an ensuing proliferation in the use of the term "discourse" in recent years (cf. Kerchner 2006b, Holzscheiter 2013). In IR, social constructivist scholars have drawn on Habermas to expand the discipline's traditional focus on rationalist-materialist explanations of agency (Risse 2000, Müller 2004), albeit without embracing the normative-critical ambition that informs Habermasian discourse ethics and further political science research strands seeking to put its concepts to work, such as, for instance, the encompassing academic field of deliberative democracy theory and research (for an overview, Elster 1998, Fischkin et al 2003, Thomson 2008). In critical security studies, proponents of Copenhagen School securitization theory have instead sought to implement an analytical-pragmatic concept of discourse derived from John Searl's theory of "speech acts" as performative linguistic agency (cf. Weaver 1995, Buzan et al 1998), as have IR social constructivists (cf. Onuf 2013). The critical discourse analysis (CDA) framework developed by scholars like Norman Fairclough and Tuen A. Djik instead uses discourse analysis as a tool for ideology critique aiming to uncover the "true" interests of social classes and other groups, hence affirming an emancipatory ambition (cf. Fairclough 2013: 21-4). Such a position in turn stands in sharp contrast with poststructuralist approaches in IR and political science more broadly that focus on the interconnectedness and indeed inextricability of language, knowledge and power, thus drawing on an anti-essentialist understanding of the possibilities and purposes of critique (Der Derian et al 1989; Ashley et al 1990; Diez 1999, Hansen 2006). Finally, post-Marxist discourse theory, as propagated by Chantal Mouffe and Ernesto Laclau, draws on both neo-Marxist, particularly Gramscian, and post-structuralist theory in seeking to combine an anti-essentialist view of knowledge and power with an emancipatory understanding of critique (Laclau/Mouffe 1990).

Rather than going into further detail in describing the overwhelming multitude of ways in which the concept of "discourse" has been employed in IR and political science, or purporting to having provided a comprehesive description of this field (for a systematic overview, cf. respectively Holzscheiter 2013 and Kerchner 2006b), the point I am seeking to illustrate is how conceptualizations of the term "discourse" differ in regard to the implied epistemological position, their understanding of sciences and hence their research interests. The epistemological spectrum in political science and IR discourse research reaches from analytical-pragmatic accounts, such as analyses drawing from Searl's "speech act" theory, to normative-critical accounts which often draw on Habermas and finally to anti-essentialist and genealogical perspectives such as post-structuralism and post-Marxism (cf. Kerchner 2006b). Moreover, drawing on the taxonomy developed by Anna Holzscheiter, usages of the term can be differentiated according to their level of analysis (micro/macro) and the presumed power–discourse relationship (deliberative/productive) (2013: 3). Drawing on these axes, a Foucauldian perspective as it is understood here can be characterized as lending itself to a macro-level analysis, while assuming a productive relationship between power and discourse, operating from a post-positivist view of science and following an anti-essentialist critical research interest (on the latter point cf. in particular Foucault 1984).

2.2 Foucauldian Discourse Analysis

Foucauldian discourse analysis hence differs significantly from both normative-critical and analytical-pragmatic perspectives (cf. Kerchner 2006a). In the Foucauldian sense of the term, discourse cannot be equated with concrete speech situations in which (exogenously given) actors participate, nor is it possible to define procedural rules by virtue of which one could approximate or determine the distance to a normative-regulatory ideal of a rational discourse free of domination. Rather, discourse as a concept serves to highlight how subjectivities and institutions of the social world are contingent on and produced by orders of knowledge that are continuously (re)produced and manifest themselves in regularities of speech and text (Foucault [1970] (2010); [1969] (1981).

Discourse analysis hence endeavors to uncover the implicit rules and exclusions which define the boundaries of what is (reasonably) speak-

and thinkable in a given historical constellation (Kerchner 2006a; Stielike 2011). It does so by seeking to describe the way in which "the production of discourse is at once controlled, selected, organized and redistributed according to a certain number of procedures" ([1970] 2010: 216). In a Foucauldian understanding, discourse is therefore not a reflection of actual or "real" political struggles, but rather both the means and end of social domination; "the very object of man's conflicts" (Foucault [1970] 2010: 216). In a similar sense, subjects do not produce discourse any more than discourse produces subjectivity through ordering and exclusion in regard to the subjects that can produce intelligible, true speech in a given context:

"Discourse is not the majestically unfolding manifestation of a thinking, knowing, speaking subject, but, on the contrary, a totality, in which the dispersion of the subject and his discontinuity with himself may be determined" ([1970] 2010: 55).

The ultimate purpose of discourse analysis, as it is understood here, is to describe the regularities of text and speech so as to make visible their contingency, power effects and mechanisms of establishing "truth" (Foucault [1970] 2010: 216). Or to put it differently, to analyze textual representation starting from the premise that the sum of sentences constituting a particular discourse inevitably reflect a *rarity*, that "everything is never said" (Foucault 1972: 119), so that an analysis of such discursive formations inherently "poses the question of power" (Foucault 1972: 120).

Following Foucault, such an endeavor has two interrelated aspects: i) genealogy and ii) critique or archeology. The genealogical technique aims to uncover the instability of contemporary perceptions by tracing the historical, discursive emergence of "problems" that pose themselves in the present (Kerchner 2011, Foucault 1977, in particular: 144-52). Foucauldian genealogy derives from a decidedly anti-essentialist view of history: it seeks to follow and disentangle the "complex course of descent" or *Herkunft* (Foucault 1977: 145). This involves "maintaining passing events in their proper dispersion" and discovering "that truth or being does not lie at the root of what we know and what we are, but the exteriority of accidents" (Foucault 1977: 146). In this sense, the genealogical method disassociates itself from any attempts at recovering the true origins of contemporary phenomena and instead emphasizes discontinuity, chance and the production of truth through power relations; "the hazardous play of domination" and emergence of problems, objects, perception and certainty as a product of "a particular stage of forces" (Foucault 1977: 148-9, cf. also 142, Kerchner 2011). Crucially, this aspect of Foucauldian discourse analysis involves what Kerchner terms a "walk to the historical archive" (Kerchner 2011: 9). That is, if taken seriously, it necessitates going beyond theoretical claims about historical contingencies to empirically investigate how contemporary orders of speech have come into being (their *Gewordensein*) by drawing on and contrasting historical text material with contemporary discursive regularities (Kerchner 2006: 24, for a discussion of genealogy as a method of critique in Foucault and Nietzsche, cf. also Saar 2008).

Archeology, or critique, is the corresponding method for describing discursive regularities and defining the rules that delineate the speakable in a given discursive constellation (cf. Foucault [1970] 2010: 230, 233; Kerchner 2006a: 29-30). As a method, archeology is described most systematically and in most detail in *The Archeology of Knowledge* (Foucault [1970] 2010). Here again, Foucault explicitly distances himself from the occupation with continuity and allegorical description, which, he argues, characterizes traditional history of thought (Diaz-Bone 1999: 124, Foucault [1970] 2010: 25-27). Along with the change in perspective that Foucault proposes, traditional concepts are suspended, such as "influence", "mentality" or "evolution", but also units such as the "book", "author" and "oeuvre" (Foucault [1970] 2010: 26). Instead, Foucault propagates an analysis that deals with textual material "in its raw neutral state, [as] a population of events in the space of discourse" (Foucault [1970] 2010: 27). The most basic, structuring units, which a thus under-stood analysis serves to uncover, are the "statements" (*enoncés*) (Foucault [1970] 2010: 31). Put it simply, a statement is an implicit, structuring assumption that determines the limits of what is reasonably speakable in the context of a given discursive formation (Foucault [1970] 2010: 106-12). Or, as Foucault puts it:

"[...] a function of existence that properly belongs to signs and on the basis of which one may then decide, through analysis or intuition, whether or not [individual sentences] 'make sense', according to what rule they follow one another, are juxtaposed, of what they are a sign and what sort of act is carried out by their formulation (oral or written)" (Foucault

[1970] 2010: 86).

Statements thus determine what sentences "make sense" and are "thinkable" in a given context. Through the unraveling description of statements, their boundaries and the relations between them, the resulting inevitable exclusion of other possible sentences are meant to be made visible. Or to put it in another way: such an analysis deals with the histor-ical emergence and contingency of taken for granted perceptions and knowledge by scrutinizing the boundaries sustaining their status as "truth". A discursive formation can be defined as a group of such state-ments whose internal relations are characterized by a certain degree of regularity (Foucault [1970] 2010: 108). This regularity, in turn, results from the "rules of formation" that the elements of discourse – discursive objects, concepts, sentences and strategies – are subject to and that enable them to appear as a part of discourse, as something nameable, something that can be talked about (cf. Foucault [1970] 2010: 40-71). The rules of formation describe a given object's relations to other discursive elements, the conditions for its "modification" and "disappearance" (Foucault [1970] 2010: 38). In short, they can be understood as conditions of "existence [...] in a given discursive division" (Foucault [1970] 2010: 38, cf. also 44-5), or, as a set of relations enabling something "to appear, to juxtapose itself to other objects, to situate itself in relation to them, to define its difference, its irreducibility, perhaps even its heterogeneity, in short to be placed in a field of exteriority" (Foucault [1970] 2010: 45).

Against this backdrop, the central research question formulated above (cf. 1.1) can be translated into a set of more specific questions that draw on different aspects of the Foucauldian theoretical "tool box" to describe discursive regularities and their borders, thus providing a more detailed guide for the primary analysis:

- How is "democracy" constituted as a discursive object in the context of contemporary EU governance, how does it relate to other objects and what discursive conditions (rules of formation) can be identified for its emergence as an intelligible part of discourse?

- What underlying statements (enoncés) can be defined that determine the limits of what is reasonably speakable in this context? What knowledge underpins discursive regularities? What position(s) of the speaking subject governs the modalities of their reproduction?

- Finally, how do contemporary orders of speech compare to regularities structuring historical text material concerned "democracy" in the context of European governance?

While the first two groups of questions can be worked on by applying an archeological analysis to contemporary text material, the third necessitates a genealogical step and hence an engagement with the historical archive.

2.3 Methodology and Text Corpus

How would one proceed to implement a Foucauldian understanding of discourse as a research methodology and what steps could one follow to provide an answer to the questions above? The first, most urgent practical question that arises in this regard concerns the delineation of a limited body of text on the basis of which the search for discursive regularities can take its course (cf. Diaz-Bone 1999: 130). What then are the relevant sites of speaking and talking about "democracy", "democratization" and "democracy promotion" as objects of EU/European governance? While one could easily imagine a variety of text corpuses that could be deemed relevant – such as documents stemming from the EU institutions themselves or texts produced by NGOs involved in democracy promotion activities – I use social science texts dealing with EU governance and EU politics as primary material for the analysis. This focus is motivated by the convergences between debates in European studies and IR with practitioner discourses on democracy as a norm or value of somewhat EU/European quality and the associated perceptions of democratization as a foreign policy objective that was discussed in the introduction and served as an initial impetus for the present investigation (cf. above, 1.1). Moreover, the analysis of scientific material seems to be very much in line with Foucault as he writes:

"in what other region do discursive events appear to be more closely linked to one another, to occur in accordance with more easily decipherable relations, than in the region usually known as science?" (Foucault [1970] 2010: 29)

In *The Order of Discourse*, Foucault talks about the "will to truth" as one of the principle mechanisms of discursive exclusion besides prohibition and the opposition between reason and madness ([1970] 2010: 54-55).

While it would certainly be problematic to assume that the will to truth is to be found in "scientific" knowledge production only, texts that are attributed with terms like "science" or "studies" nevertheless seem to constitute a particularly prolific site for studying processes of valorizing and verifying knowledge. That is, I suspect that rules determining whether or not a given sentence advancing a claim about democracy can gain the status of truth in the context of contemporary EU/European governance might be studied in social science disciplines concerned with explaining and measuring the latter as an empirical reality.

Furthermore, a focus on social science literature is interesting given the fact that the role of science and academia in the discursive production of knowledge about EU/European governance has often received much less attention than practices and texts produced by EU institutions, civil society or in "cultural" spheres (for an exception, cf. Diez 1999). In IR, the influence of knowledge on governance practices has received some attention through the strand of scholarship associated with the term "epistemic communities". This concept is based around the argument that international "policy coordination" and cooperation is based on mutual expectations amongst actors in the sense of shared perceptions of problems and solutions in international politics that derive:

"from interpretive processes involving political and cultural structures, as well as from institutions dedicated to defining and modifying values and the meaning of action" (Adler / Haas 1992: 371).

While the present study reflects a similar interest in the sense that it directs attention to perception, it also occupies a more self-reflexive position by looking at knowledge within the social sciences themselves, rather than at technical expertise in international governance and specific communities of experts, as scholars within the "epistemic community" research agenda have preponderantly done (cf. Cross 2013). As a further difference between a Foucauldian perspective and the "epistemic comunities" approach, it might be pointed out that the latter, including the innovations to the framework recently proposed by Mai'a K Davis Cross, investigates "how knowledge translates into power" via the empowerment of "knowledge-based actors and networks" (Cross 2013: 138). It therefore draws on an understanding of power as a capacity of actors and knowledge as a means of power exertion. A Foucauldian understanding of the relationship of knowledge and power instead looks at "power *of* discourse" (Holzscheiter 2011: 5, emphasis added), e.g. the power effects inherent to knowledge production and orders of speech through exclusion and productive effects.

In this respect, the field of research referred to as "Actor-Network-Theory" (ANT), but more accurately described as "sociology of science" (Latour 2013: 9-10), and to some extent also the related growing interdisciplinary field of Science and Technology Studies (STS), might have more in common with a Foucauldian, discourse-analytical approach using social science texts as primary research material. ANT has been described as an "anti-method" and "non-theory" (cf. Rowland et al 2011: 98), as it sets out from a cartography of how the social sciences – in particular sociology and "sociological" explanation in other social science fields – divide and give rise to the "social" as an object of knowledge, a specific domain of society (Latour 2013: 21-6, Law et al 1999). ANT scholars criticize the performative, reifying effects of such theorizing and instead propagate an analysis that traces "controversies about associations without restricting in advance the social to a specific domain", thereby rendering "traceable the means allowing actors to stabilize those controversies" with the goal of "reassembl[ing] the social not in a society but in a collective" (Latour 2013: 14). The present investigation can thus be seen to draw on a similar interest in the ordering, productive and reifying effects of social science discourse, yet by employing a Foucauldian approach it is more "modest" in its ambitions in the sense that it restricts itself to the study of social science discourse, rather than aiming at any substantial "reassembling" exercise of the units of discourse it seeks to uncover.

Finally, the expanding academic field of STS research also attests to the relevance and increasing scholarly interest in studying science as a part of society that has arisen in recent years, albeit mainly outside of the IR, European studies and political science disciplinary boundaries. As STS is by now a markedly diverse field of research, this is not the place to elaborate on its composition in any greater detail (for such an overview cf. Sismondo 2009). Here, it suffices to maintain that STS scholars start from a critical, post-positivist perspective on scientific and technical knowledge formation as social activities that unfold constitutive effects (Sismondo 2009: 3-12, Collins et al 1998). Hence, STS shares the self-reflexive stance on scientific knowledge production that is propagated here and, in consequence, provides a further argument in favor of the choice of social science texts as primary material for the analysis.

With these things in mind, the text corpus consists of a series of social science texts. More specifically, I have chosen to look at the 2004–2014 editions of the Journal of Common Market Studies (JCMS). The JCMS has provided an authoritative source of analysis on various dimensions of European politics and integration since the 1960s. It publishes contributions by prominent IR, European integration and political theory scholars, but also contributions by leading EU practitioners. During the investigated time span, members of the European Commission, the European Parliament and the president of the Commission, José Manuel Barroso, were amongst the contributors. The texts hence oscillate between empiricist social science, normative-philosophical accounts, legal argumentation and more practical considerations bordering on policy advice. Without making any far-reaching claims about representativity, I would nevertheless argue that the JCMS provides for an interesting and relevant source of material due to the central position that the journal seems to occupy within discursive fields of knowledge production about governance and politics in the EU. As a method for reducing the number of articles to be analyzed in greater detail, I used the search words "democracy" and "democratic" in the JCMS database to delineate a corpus of a total of 134 individual articles and around 50 reviews. That is, all articles mentioning democracy during the past ten years were included in the more in-depth, archeological analysis. Besides practical considerations and the JCMS' authoritative position at the nexus of the social sciences and EU governance practice, the concrete choice of material was further motivated by the assumption that the relative high number of authors and thus of (seemingly) different perspectives and lines of argumentation provides for a sufficiently broad, appropriate basis to define underlying statements and borders that characterize general orders of speech in the field (cf. Stielike 2012). For the sake of simplicity I cite the text corpus by year and page number, instead of the customary citation by author, year, title of the article, "In:" title of the publication, issue and page numbers. This choice was made for practical reasons due to the high number of articles however, it is also informed by the understanding that taking on a Foucauldian discourse-analytical perspective involves a move towards suspending the "author" as the central point of analysis or the natural unit of texts (cf. above 2.2, Foucault [1970] 2010: 26, Kerchner 2006c). While such a change in perspective, ideally, enables one to discern the borders of a discursive constellation, it also blackens out and is ill suited to account for the nuances of arguments, theories, methods and findings that separate individual authors and scholars. There are various methods of discourse and text analysis within political science which are much more suitable for such tasks, including analytical-pragmatic discourse analysis, CDA or Habermasian approaches. Foucauldian methodology, in the way that it is understood here, does not intend to de-qualify other approaches or individual scholars by disregarding the author as a central category of text analysis, but instead represents an attempt to follow another – perhaps more unusual – kind or question which concerns the broader patterns of textuality and its borders, rather than actors, authors, agency, interaction and differences in positions internal to a given discursive context.

On this basis of the JCMS text corpus, I thus seek to investigate in more detail what regularities, exclusions and borders of what is (reasonably) speakable might be seen to govern contemporary discourses that constitute "democracy" as a discursive object, what underlying assumptions stabilize such perceptions and how it relates to other discursive elements. To do so, I apply a rather straightforward approach to archeological description that draws on *The Archeology of Knowledge* by proceeding from the rules of formation to the definition of statements and finally to a discussion of the relations between the defined regularities, rules and borders. This procedure draws on the sequence of argumentation in *The Archeology of Knowledge* but also on Brigitte Kerchner's proposal for operationalizing Foucauldian discourse analysis along the lines of seven central questions (2010: 11). Also following Kerchner (2010), the discussion of the rules of formation (cf. below, 3.1) concentrates on the enunciative modalities (cf. below, 3.14) and the formation of objects. The latter includes an analysis of the discursive field and its authorities of delimitation (cf. below, 3.11), recurring equations, opposition and grids of specification that order objects in relationship to each other (cf. below, 3.12) and the ordering effects of assigning objects to more comprehensive systems, such as state/society or politics/economy (cf. below, 3.13). The definition and discussion of statements draws closely on *The Archeology of Knowledge* in describing statements along the lines of four dimensions:

the “referential”, the “associated domain”, the “subject position” and the “repeatable materiality” (Foucault [1970] 2010: 88-105, cf. below, 3.2).

By proceeding in this way, I therefore single out a more limited set of theoretical concepts amongst the multitude presented in *The Archeology of Knowledge* to constitute the analytical focus of the investigation. For instance, I do not conduct a systematic analysis of the formation of concepts. This would have included a consideration of how concepts are brought into order in relationship to each other through “forms of succession”, “types of dependence”, “forms of coexistence” and possible ways of “combining” concepts (Foucault [1970] 2010: 56-8) as well as of different “procedures of intervention” (Foucault [1970] 2010: 57-8). In my reading, a systematic analysis of these aspects of textual regularities would come close to an archeological analysis of the social sciences as such, thus going well beyond the scope of the present master thesis. Therefore, these aspects do not constitute a separate analytical step, but instead are touched upon throughout the analysis when deemed relevant for the constitution of “democracy” as a discursive object.

The archeological analysis of JCMS’ text corpus constitutes the main bulk of the investigation. However, in order to provide a contrast and possibly subvert the naturalness of the perceptions and regularities that the main analysis uncovers, in a second step, I also use historical texts that were articulated before the point where their perceived quality as something obviously true/existent was consolidated. Hereby, I draw on Siegfried Jäger's proposal for implementing historical discourse analysis by singling out diachronic, temporally rather widely dispersed sections of text in the thread of discourse in order to identify continuities and breaches in perceptions and regularities over the course of time (cf. Jäger 2001: 102-3). The second text corpus consists of material from 19th-century classical liberal political philosophy: John Stuart Mill's “On Liberty” (1859) and “Considerations on Representative Government” (1861), Benjamin Constant's “De la liberté des Anciens comparée à celle des Modernes” (1819) and Alexis de Tocqueville's “Democracy in America” (1835). These texts resemble the JCMS text material in the sense that they are equally concerned with the question of defining legitimate, just forms of government, of understanding the workings of state and society and how it relates to “democracy”. Furthermore, the choice of material also draws on Hobson's observations about the “unlikely marriage” between liberalism and democracy in the 20th century (see above, 1.3) and the writings by post-Marxist theorist Chantal Mouffe, who has, similarly, investigated the historical emergence of this discursive connection and emphasizes its contingency and historical and logical non-necessity (Laclau/Mouffe 1990: 230-41, Mouffe 2000). This second step of analysis hence provides for a genealogical perspective, a historical gaze on the present articulations found in the JCMS texts through an excursion into the archives of European thought on the art of government. To put it differently, it seeks to disentangle some aspects of the "complex course of descent" (Foucault 1977: 145), to grasp the historical specificity of contemporary perceptions and the disparity and impurity of their "numberless beginnings" (Foucault 1977: 145).

A final remark on the limits of the investigation. As Foucault notes, the "historical conditions required if one is to 'say anything' " are indeed "many and imposing" (Foucault [1970] 2010: 44). Thus, the present analysis cannot be regarded as exhaustive in regard to the conditions that let objects, theories, themes, concepts, subjectivities and so forth emerge and position themselves in relation to other elements. Rather, it represents an attempt to make use of Foucauldian methodology while singling out certain aspects of its "toolbox" to provide an interpretation of the guiding questions formulated above. Furthermore, a Foucauldian approach as such also implies the exclusion of a multitude of other possible questions that one could ask about the same material or the same objects of discourse. Inter alia, by seeking to define the borders of contemporary speech, internal variations that could be the object of other kinds of discourse research are necessarily blinded out.

3 Democracy in Contemporary EU Governance: An Archeological Statement Analysis

3.1 Rules of Formation

3.1.1 *The Discursive Field and Authorities of Delimitation*

In order to uncover the rules of formation in a given amount of text, Foucault proposes to start by mapping the formation of objects. Here, "the first surfaces of emergence" are to be considered and described before proceeding to the "authorities of delimitation" and "grids of specification" (Foucault [1970] 2010: 41-2). Authorities of delimitation, he maintains, are social institutions that "delimit, designate, name and establish [something] as an object", while grids of specification are systems according to which objects are "divided, contrasted, related, regrouped, classified [and] derived from one another" (Foucault [1970] 2010: 42). Brigitte Kerchner reformulates these methodological points of attack as follows: "How do scientific disciplines constitute things and persons in their mutual relations by defining, grouping and assigning them to comprehensive systems (such as culture/nature, society and politics)?" (2011: 10). In order to embark on an archeological description of the sentences in the text corpus, the question thus poses itself in what "field of objects" (Gehring 2006: 172) the term "democracy" emerges, how these objects are ordered, what social authorities and discursive boundaries lend them a sense of certainty.

Throughout the time span covered by the JCMS text corpus, mentions of "democracy" surface as parts of an encompassing, seemingly fragmented field of objects. Central elements include analytical, descriptive categories from the fields of IR and European studies research – such as "compliance", "conditionality", "diffusion", "competences", "capabilities", "actorship", "international role"/"identity", "normative power", "EU norms"/"values", "Europeanization", political system "sui generis", "intergovernmentalism", "supranationalism" or "multi-level governance". Objects stemming from knowledge production about political systems, political philosophy and law also frequently appear, including for instance "citizen(ship)", "electorate", "election", "political parties", "leaders", "responsibility", "accountability", "(human) rights", "(democratic) legitimacy", "the rule of law", "constitution", "checks and balances", "demos", "European"/"common collective identity" or "public opinion". Finally, vocabulary drawing on, or intersecting with, economic disciplines and statistical, quantitive ordering and truth procedures is noticeable in terms such as competition", "market economy", "performance", "liberalization", "effectiveness", "input", "output", "equilibrium", "scores", "variables" or "indicators".

What authorities of delimitation (Foucault [1970] 2010: 41-2) can be said to establish democracy as an object that can be talked about in this context, to lend certainty to its existence and the field of objects where it appears? The above categories of objects and the way that they are ordered in the texts seem to reflect a series of related boundaries and rules, within which truth can be established; a regularity or pattern of possible ways of "combining" and "ordering" concepts (Foucault [1970] 2010: 56-7). There is a recurring concern with the correct or "valid" conceptual description and "unbiased" statistical representation of empirically given entities and their distribution. The uncovering of causal relations through targeted variation and non-variation of separable "factors", "dependent" and "independent variables", to measure "influ-ence" on outcomes represent a further point of interest and inquiry (for an illustration, cf. for instance JCMS 2012: 972 or JCMS 2014: 870)[2]. Taken together, one can thus discern an occupation with the isolation of the "political fact" and its "reasons". Other sentences instead aim at normative definitions of procedures for generating and according "legitimacy" to governance techniques and institutions (for instance JCMS 2007: 528; JCMS 2008: 104; JCMS 2012: 510-3). Yet other articulations stem from a preoccupation with efficiency and its measurement as a continuous search for improving and enhancing given sets of societal relations and mechanisms. Hence, the social sciences as a societal institution seem to me to constitute the most relevant sources of authority that delimit, designate, name and establish democracy and related objects, hence defining what kind of sentences belong to discourse, and what kinds do not. Moreover, the fact that "democracy" constitutes such a paramount object of inquiry in such a large number of social science disciplines – including in particular political science, IR, economics, legal theory and social and political philoso-

---

2 For the sake of simplicity and due to the high number of articles analyzed and cited, I referenced the JCMS text material by year and pages number (cf. above 2.3).

phy – can be seen to attest to an overarching perception of urgency and importance to fixate its meaning and lend certainty to its content.

3.1.2 *Equations, Opposition and Grids of Specification*

How is this multitude of objects in the texts ordered in relationship to each other through contrasts, connections and groupings (Foucault [1970] 2010: 42) and to what extent can such patterns be said to delineate the speakble about "democracy" in our text corpus? If one sets out to map the relations between objects that recur in explicit and implicit forms across the texts, one is soon confronted with a proliferation of such relationships. At the same time, going along with the Foucauldian framework in assuming that textual relations between objects, such as the opposition between "democracy" and "dictatorship" which is repeated across the texts, represent contingent, productive dichotomizations rather than names or signs describing a reality that exists outside of speech, might render seemingly "shocking" results, as it serves the purpose of deconstructing and thus puts into question the ordering oppositions that are usually taken for granted in both social science and everyday political practices (cf. Kerchner 2006c). This also means that we ought to be careful in claiming too much, too soon when observing a textual pattern of opposition, connection or equation. That is, any claim about what dichotomizations serve as boundaries for the reasonably speakable requires careful consideration and extensive text analysis. Hence, in this section I sketch out some of the patterns of opposition and connection between objects that present themselves upon careful analysis of the text corpus. However, rather than advancing any definite claims about their character as discursive boundaries outside of which speech would no longer be intelligible or become mere noise in the context of the JCMS text corpus, this exercise serves the more modest purpose of identifying indications pointing towards such findings and of introducing some further elements circulating in the texts, while outlining patterns of connections and oppositions in order to start encircling some of the discursive borders which the further archeological chapters study in more detail. Due to the multitude of relations, the later chapters necessarily look at some of the patterns that I touch upon below in greater detail than others, hence also leaving the other connections and contrasts as starting points for future research to inquire about more systematically. Moreover, rather than postulating any conclusions about the historical contingency of connections and dichotomization in contemporary speech on the basis of theoretical deduction, such claims are carefully substantiated with regard to a few selected points later on through the genealogical excursion that follows the archeological analysis (see below chapter 4).

Against the backdrop of these limitations and clarifications, let us return to the concrete task of text analysis. To bring some structure to the proliferation of relations between objects or "grids of specification" that make up the scene where "democracy" appears, let us first consider connections and equations. Across the variety of sentences that make reference to "democracy" in the text corpus, the term is often connected or equated with a series of discursive objects referring to specific kinds of political institutions and social relations. Most notably, democracy is frequently seen to consist of, or be contingent upon, "representation", "free and fair elections", "political competition", "(party) pluralism", "accountability" of "political leaders"/"elites", "openness"/ "transparency" and a "strong" /"independent civil society" (cf. inter alia JCMS 2006: 45; JCMS 2007: 58; JCMS 2008: 109, 156; JCMS 2009: 20, 22, 37, 628; JCMS 2010: 222, 653, 654, 670, 737, 906, 1044, 1059, 1092, 1265; JCMS 2011: 499, 654, 999, 1047; JCMS 2012: 88, 90, 372, 379). Moreover, democracy is often closely connected to or seen to necessitate "basic", "natural", "human", "individual" rights, the rights of "minority groups" (JCMS 2005: 189; JCMS 2009: 902; JCMS 2010: 765) and a range of further objects that are repeatedly perceived to generate a "balance", "equilibrium" or "reconciliation" of interests, to prevent "con-centration" and "abuse" of power and to obviate political conflict from "degenerating into [...] intense polarization" (JCMS 2010: 745; JCMS 2012: 192, 794). The latter group usually includes processes of "scrutiny", "oversight" and "control" of leaders and institutions by "opposition" parties, "independent civil society" actors, by "free media" and also between political institutions in the form of "parliamentary control of the executive" or the "separation of powers" (JCMS 2005: 33, 165; JCMS 2008: 15, 108, 156; JCMS 2009: 691; JCMS 2010: 745; JCMS 2012: 793; JCMS 2014: 140). In different individual sentences distributed across the texts, democracy is seen to profit from or to attain a "higher quality" through connections with objects like "participation", "deliberation", "a dynamic public sphere", and also with a strong "sense of community", "collective identity" or "demos" (JCMS 2004: 993-4; JCMS 2008: 455; JCMS 2010: 906; JCMS 2012: 786, 792; JCMS 2013: 340). These objects, in turn, are often seen in conjuncture with "stability", "strength" and "trust" in "political institutions" and "elites" (JCMS 2005: 163; JCMS 2012: 367, 789; JCMS 2013: 593). To illustrate:

"The trust hypothesis' two component assumptions – that democracy needs trust and that communal identifications can strengthen trust – enjoy solid theoretical and empirical backing." (JCMS 2012: 790)

Moreover, as a recurring pattern democracy figures in close proximity to objects with conspicuously normative connotations: "justice", "legitimacy", "freedom", "peace", "trust", "stability", "human rights", "development", "good governance", "growth" and "prosperity". These relationships are frequently understood in terms of "mutually reinforcing factors" (2008: 901), with the said objects constituting either the consequence of democracy or alternatively a condition for "high quality" democracy to emerge (JCMS 2006: 665; JCMS 2007: 48, 58; JCMS 2008: 20, 901; JCMS 2009: 20, 919; JCMS 2010: 740; JCMS 2011: 997, 1002; JCMS 2012: 519, 589, 618). For instance, it is asserted that "democracies, despite conflicts, do not attack each other", that democracy leads to "increased welfare and economic exchange" and the avoidance of "instability and bad governance" (JCMS 2010: 996). A sense of certainty that democracy entails a close causal relation with other objects that are perceived to be normatively or morally desirable might hence constitute a textual regularity, while the nature of these relationships (does peace facilitate democracy or democracy lead to peace, and how?) constitutes points of uncertainty and divergence.

Finally, connections between the "EU" or "Europe", on the one hand, and "democracy", "democratic principles" etc., on the other, often occur. This pattern is particularly frequent in sentences concerned with EU external relations and the international realm. Here, objects such as "democratization", "democracy promotion", "democracy assistance" or "democracy export" appear interchangeably as characterizations of EU foreign policy techniques and objectives, but also as constituent "values", "norms" or "principles" that are perceived to make up the EU's "foreign policy identity" and define the "soft", "civilian", "normative", "values-based" or "ethical" nature of the power and influence which the Union exerts internationally (JCMS 2005: 189; JCMS 2007: 515, 517; JCMS 2010: 582; JCMS 2011: 997). In this context, "democratization" and "democracy promotion" are often seen in close conjuncture with terms referring to political-economical transformative processes such as "Europeanization", "Westernization", "development", "transition", "institutional adjustment", "reform" or "liberalization" (cf. JCMS 2006: 39, 45, 217; JCMS 2007: 517, 526; JCMS 2010: 582). A further, related group of objects describes the different techniques that EU institutions employ in order to induce such change. These encompass, inter alia, "normative suasion", "socialization", "naming and shaming", "political conditionality", "capacity"/"institution building" and "civil society empowerment" (JCMS 2004: 222; JCMS 2005: 189; JCMS 2006: 43, 749; JCMS 2007: 48, 251; JCMS 2010: 593; JCMS 2011: 490, 995, 997; JCMS 2013: 807).

Beyond this accumulation of connections and equations, a series of oppositions between "democracy" and other objects recur throughout the text material. While "democratic systems", "democratic countries", "democratic states" or "democratic government" are often seen as opposed to "authoritarianism", "autocracy", "dictatorship" and "communism", terms such as "democratic society", "democratic values" and "democratic priciples" that refer to beliefs or norms rather than formal aspects of governance institutions are instead contrasted with terms such as "nationalism", "(Islamic) fundamentalism", "closed-mindedness", "populism" or "political extremism" in different sentences spread across the corpus (JCMS 2004: 1667; JCMS 2006: 534; JCMS 2008: 691, 912; JCMS 2009: 691; JCMS 2012: 379, 589, 793; JCMS 2014: 105, 861, 866).

These oppositions, in turn, are often connected with and described in terms of conceptual pairs such as "open" / "closed" (state or society), "transparent"/"secretive", "accountability"/"impunity", "responsible"/ "populist", "responsibility"/"blame-shifting", "citizens' trust"/ "abstentionism", "trust in elites"/"cynicism", "efficiency"/"bureaucracy", "performance"/"corruption", "tolerance"/"xenophobia", "tolerant"/ "illiberal", "neutrality"/"ideology" (JCMS 2004: 991; JCMS 2005: 222; JCMS 2006: 545; JCMS 2010: 582, 743; JCMS 2011: 184; JCMS 2012: 629; JCMS 2014: 138, 140, 391). Here, the interconnected contrasts between "democracy", on the one hand, and "populism" or "extremism", on the other, which in the text corpus repeat themselves across units such as sentences, years and articles, seem to me to be of particular interest with regard to the question of what constitutes the boundaries of "democracy" as an object. Both concepts are associated with formulations such as "lacking trust in national governments as well as in EU institutions" or "general cynicism about national leaders" (JCMS 2004: 990-1; JCMS 2006: 746). Whereas "extremism" is understood as pertaining to both "left" and "right" positions "far away" from an imagined middle of the "political spectrum" (cf. JCMS 2005: 166; JCMS 2014: 861, 886), populism is explained to be a "division of society along a single [...] cleavage dividing the good people from some evil establishment" (JCMS 2014: 391). I will discuss this point in greater detail later on (cf. below 3.23). For now, however, let us proceed to some further oppositions between objects in the texts that recur in our text corpus.

As a further pattern, we can identify a series of identity descriptions. Here, "the EU", "Europe" and "the West" are often understood to constitute "first world democracies", "developed industrial democracies" or "advanced democracies", and as such are repeatedly contrasted with categories such as "transitional countries", "target countries", "postcommunist systems", "regimes", "emerging democracies", "grey-zone democracies" or "reluctant democratizers" (JCMS 2005: 185, 190; JCMS 2007: 521, 526; JCMS 2008: 20). This textual pattern might be seen to imply positive/negative connotations, or a sense of hierarchy between identity description. Such suppositions are strengthened by the recurring formulation of "grading systems" or "indexes" which assign different "democracy scores" or "polity scores" to countries and regions based on their "level" of democracy and political freedom (cf. for instance: JCMS 2004: 213; JCMS 2006: 44; JCMS 2010: 743; JCMS 2012: 621) and recurrence of formulations asserting that "countries differ in their stage of maturity towards the [democratic] values the EU seeks to promote" (JCMS 2006: 43) or maintaining that "we need to set benchmarks to measure what we expect our neighbors to do in order to advance from one stage to another" (JCMS 2005: 33).

3.1.3 *Ordering Effects of Comprehensive Systems*

Before turning to the enunciative modalities and the question of "who is speaking" this magnitude of sentences, I would like to touch upon a few underlying distinctions that seem to be of particular relevance in delineating the perception of what democracy entails and in structuring the discursive field where it appears by "assigning [things] to comprehensive systems" (Kerchner 2010:11). For instance, the constitution of "politics" and "the economy" as separate societal spheres which follow different logics and ought to be judged by different criteria seems to me to serves as an underlying discursive prerequisite for democracy to be understood as a category that is relevant to the design of "political institutions", to processes that take place in relation to them or for understanding how they interact with society, but not, say, to the working place or the distribution of wealth and property. At times, democracy figures as a source of "regulation" or "intervention" into the economic sphere, but it is never perceived to constitute a principle, an ideal, a criteria or a procedure according to which economic processes *as such* can be judged, or descriptive knowledge about their empirical reality can be produced. Instead, the term "democracy" is understood as a description of a certain kind of political system, thus relying on and being circumscribed by a discursive constitution of "the economy" and "the market" as pre-political, given entities; as separable societal spheres and logics. To give a concrete example, this regularity is reflected in the recurring concept of "market distortion" (cf. JCMS 2011: 495, 1100). A perception that the market becomes "distorted" by political "interventions" implicitly assumes an understanding of market mechanism as such as quasi-natural phenomena – as having been *un*distorted prior to intervention and thus as unfolding a natural logic separate from and independent of the political sphere of human affairs. Here, a similar discursive logic to what Burron (2011, 2012) described as a discursive naturalization of market processes in US-American democracy promotion seems to be at work. Although, however, there is no unequivocal "political code that restricts democratic control over the economy and sanctifies the logic of the market" (Burron 2012: 1658); rather, there is an assumption that the market *has* a specific (pre-political) logic that is separable from the logics of politics and thus of democracy.

A second distinction that I would argue lends certainty and structure to the constellation of discursive objects just discussed is the division between "the state" in the sense of state institutions, and "society". Notably, "power", and consequently also its abuse, is largely attributed to nation-state or EU institutions, agencies, individual mandate holders and political parties. Society instead figures as a target of power exertion and also, in shape of "civil society", as a check and an instance that scrutinizes and limits state power and fights its abuse by demanding "accountability". Hence, articulations echoing the perception that "civil society" must be "strong" and independent of the state in democratic political system make for a notable continuity throughout the texts. At times, this leads to rather interesting problems that illustrate the ambiguity of democracy promotion through civil society funding /strengthening. In the following quote, EU governance techniques aiming to promote democracy through financial support to civil society organi-zations are criticized on the grounds that funding comes from EU "state" institutions:

"How independent are the civil-society organizations beloved by the European Commission?', asks the *Economist*. During the last few years, public funding of civil society organizations (CSOs) has almost always been subject to controversy. [...] given their strong dependence on public funds, CSOs receiving European Union (EU) support are often dubbed 'government puppets'or 'friends of the EU." (JCMS 2014: 337)

Finally, a third, related distinction can be identified in the opposition between "public" and "private". Like the above distinctions, it functions as an underlying division that contributes to delineating the sphere in which "democratic principles" are seen to be applicable. For instance, whereas the equality of citizens in the sense of formal political rights is considered to be at the very core of democracy, there are no mentions of democracy as being in any way a relevant category for an analysis or understanding of power asymmetries and abuse in personal or family relations due to gender, sex, race or other factors, all of which are understood as unacceptable grounds for discrimination in the public realm.

Taken together, I believe it can be argued that these oppositions – politics/economy, state/society, public/private – correspond with and reinforce an underlying equation between the political and the "political system". In such an understanding, politics appears as a separate domain of society which encompasses the state apparatus, political parties and to a certain extent interest groups "channelling" societal demands to the political sphere. Rather than as an act of instituting discursive borders (Lefort 1990: 282-3), the articulation of an agonistic conflictuality (Mouffe 2007: 29-30), or any other alternative conception of what politics of the political might mean, here it is understood as a place or a sector, thus making it distinguishable and separate from other entities such as culture, the market or the family. Claude Lefort has described this kind of discursive division and its connection to objectivist conceptions of science more eloquently, as follows:

"The criterion of what is political is supplied by the criterion of what is *non-political*, by the criterion of what is economic, social, juridical, aesthetic, or religious. This operation is not innocent; it hides behind a truism borrowed from the domain constituted as that of exact knowledge: sciences deals only with particulars." (Lefort [1981] 2006: 151)

3.1.4 *The Enunciative Modalities*

Besides the questions about the discursive field of objects, authorities of delimitation, grids of specification or patterns of equation and opposition and the ordering effect of comprehensive systems, which we have already touched upon, Foucault's discussion of the rules of formation in *The Archeology of Knowledge* introduces the concept of "enunciative modalities" by posing the question "Who is speaking?" (Foucault [1970] 2010: 50). Now, what more exactly, does providing an answer to such a question in a Foucauldian sense involve? Most theoretical perspectives and methodologies in political science and IR would make the answer dependent on concrete speech situation, attribute claims and sentences to actors participating therein or search for the individual author of a given passage of text. Foucault's concept of enunciative modalities, or for that sake of the subject position which we will touch upon later (3.2), however aims at a rather different aspect of speech which, once more, is located at its border and targets mechanisms of exclusion instead of accounting for internal differences between actors or authors. Rather than asking what individual subject uttered a given sentence, the question of interest in Foucauldian methodology is "who is qualified to do so?" (Foucault [1970] 2010: 50). That is, the enunciative modalities can be understood as discursive rules that describe the position from which *any* given subject would able to reproduce a given discourse or regularity in text or speech. Going along with Foucault on this point therefore involves asking how one would have to be perceived in order to produce intelligible, authoritative speech in a given context.

Let us then, take a step back and ask this question to our text corpus. The sentences figuring in the corpus could be said to derive a sense of certainty that they belonging to the same kind of speech from knowledge about the workings of society, the state, law, economy, history and/or culture and the borders separating such objects and spheres. Hence, in order to speak intelligible sentences about "democracy" and EU governance in the context of the texts that make up our corpus, one would have to occupy a discursive, social position of a subject who disposes over and has a privileged access to these domains: the position of a social scientist. In order to describe the modalities and rules delineating subject positions, Foucault proposes to ask what relationship such speaking subjects maintain to the groups of objects that populate discursive articulations; is s/he a "questioning", "listening", "seeing" subject? (cf. Foucault [1970] 2010: 51). Here, if we attempt to answer the question in general terms, the social scientist position, on the one hand, appears as a "seeing" and "observing" subject: As someone who is concerned with the valid description, proper measurement and statistical representation of socio-political empirical facts and realities, and anxious about avoiding any interaction that could deteriorate her/his results (JCMS 2004: 1069, JCMS 2007: 522, JCMS 2008: 543). On the other hand, s/he generally seeks to uncover regularities in the causal interaction between established facts, to determine "the relative importance of factors" (JCMS 2011: 998) for a specific societal outcome or to fixate what "factors account for variation" (JCMS 2012: 21). That is, s/he seeks to separate between cause and consequence. To do so, knowledge production procedures involve the combination of variation and non-variation of factors: the analysis of the spacial and/or temporal distribution of "variables" in order to trace, reconstruct causality through an imagined, retrospective "experimental verification" (Foucault [1970] 2010: 50).

In the texts, the social scientist position borders on the further one, which could be described by the term "practitioner". Subjects speaking by virtue of being perceived as, or occupying a discursive position as practitioners in European and/or international affairs regularly appear in the textual margins of the JCMS editions, for instance as reviewers of academic work judging its usefulness to practices governance, as imagined recipients or audience for the results of academic research or as occasional contributors (cf. for instance: JCMS 2003: 203, JCMS 2007: 530, JCMS 2008: 900, JCMS 2013: 810). How could his/her relationship to discursive objects be described, what kind of speech does s/he produce? Once more focusing on general boundaries rather than internal differences, what unities the position of practitioners throughout the texts could be said to be that s/he usually speaks/writes in an evaluative manner and derives her/his authority to speak about "democracy" and other objects from his/her more direct access to the practice of EU governance as the "empirical reality" constituting the object of inquiry. In addition, both subjects speaking by virtue of being perceived as "social scientists" and as "practitioners" also produce an advising, evaluative kind of speech in the texts, where "challenges" posing themselves to society, the economy or political leaders are defined, the efficiency of societal arrangements or governance practices is measured and normative criteria defining "good governance", "best practices" or moral, normative "fairness" applied to social reality. Finally, from what "institutional sites" could the speech produced by scientists and practitioners be said to "derive its legitimacy" (Foucault [1970] 2010: 50)? While the status of the scholar is confirmed by a web of academic institutions – the university, research projects, degrees and academic titles, text production and distribution: journals, books, reviews etc. – the practitioner's status as a speaking subject is established and confirmed by her/his personal, professional affiliation with EU and/or nation state governance institutions (cf. Foucault [1970] 2010: 50).

If we follow Foucault's lead in describing the enunciative modalities and posing the question "who speaks?" to our text corpus in a way that abandons the individual author and actor as its natural point of reference and unity, we derive an interesting, but perhaps also slightly simplistic picture. In the above variations, the scholar or academic appears to be defined as a speaking subject by her/his distance to the societal objects of inquiry. That is, the distance and non-affiliation with the object of which s/he speaks function as conditions for him/her to see and speak the "truth" about them. In sentences concerned with normative questions, this position is epitomized in the (Rawlsian) "veil of ignorance" where imagined subjects who do *not* "know their social position" (2013: 342) are deemed to be able to reason truthfully about the just, fair organization of society. Interestingly, this stands in stark contrast to the more marginal position of the practitioner who, on the contrary, derives his/her ability to speak truth about objects from his/her involvement with and proximity to their "empirical" existence. The reverse side of applying such an interpretation of the question "who speaks", of course, is the blackening out of internal differences between authors. Hence, this point of our analysis might be seen to illustrate both some of the advantages and risks inherent to our theoretical methodological framework: as the borders delineating orders of speech become visible, the internal variations within textuality are blurred (cf. Kerchner 2006c). As the present context is not the place to provide an exhaustive discussion of such delicate questions of methodological pros, cons and trade-offs, I believe it is more adequate to welcome a discussion on the indicated points and, for now, to proceed to the next step of our analysis.

3.2 From Sentences to Statements

After having described some of the various relations to other discursive elements that the term "democracy" entails in the text corpus and moreover, upon having touched upon a few discursive division and enunciative conditions enabling democracy "to appear, to juxtapose itself to other objects" (Foucault [1970] 2010: 45), the next step of archeological analysis is the definition and discussion of statements (enoncés). Now, within the muddled multitude of individual sentences, how does one proceed to define articulations which serve as implicit, structuring assumptions and delineate the limits of what is reasonably "speakable"? To put this rather ambitious-sounding task in more concrete, manageable terms, I believe it is useful to consider as a guiding question or strategy, what perceptions and/or assumptions can be defined that are common to seemingly opposite positions within the relevant discursive formation (cf. Stielike 2009). That is: What assumptions about "democracy" and related discursive objects and concepts are shared by different authors and positions? What borders serve as implicit conditions of diverging articulations?

As to the description of statements, Foucault specifies four dimensions or characterizing rules: the "referential", the "associated domain", the "subject position" and the "repeatable materiality" (Foucault [1970] 2010: 88-105). As statements are not reflections of non-discursive materiality, but productive truth-establishing propositions, the elements they contain cannot be understood in terms of signifiers, or names for outside elements, but rather as conditions for their unity and reproduction. Accordingly, the referential is not something external that the statement is referring to or describing (in the sense of a referent), but instead defines the epistemic, discursive conditions for the statement to emerge. It is "made up" of "laws of possibility, rules of existence for the objects that are named, designated or described within [the statement], and for the relations that are affirmed or denied" and defines "the possibilities of appearance and delimitation of that which gives meaning to the sentence, a value as truth to the proposition" (Foucault [1970] 2010: 91). In my understanding, the concept of the referential is therefore closely related to the rules of formation, equations, dichotomizations and attribution to comprehensive systems that govern the elements contained in a given statement. The associated domain instead refers to the constellation of other articulations in which a "sentence or series of signs" inscribes itself, which implicitly or explicitly draws upon and which thereby allows for it to be perceived as a intelligible part of "a particular context" and as having a "specific, representative content" (Foucault [1970] 2010: 98). It can thus, in my reading, be reformulated as the latent, associated knowledge context that a recurring sentence or assumption refers back to and that does, as a consequence, turn it into a statement. The subject position can be understood as the function, the discursive location that any given subject must occupy in order to reproduce a specific statement (Foucault [1970] 2010: 95-6). As I understand the concept it is therefore identical to the enunciative modalities discussed above, except that it poses the question of "who is qualified" to speak with regard to a specific statement rather than with a view to a discursive constellation as a whole. Lastly, the concept of "repeatable materiality" serves to indicate how the existence of a statement is dependent on being re-instituted in material, sense-perceptible elements – "who can speak of a statement if a voice had not articulated it, if a surface did not bear its sign?" (Foucault [1970] 2010: 100) – and at the same time preserves its identity as one despite the spatial-temporal dispersion of material expressions, thus being "re-peatable".

In the following, I identify four statements as textual regularities structuring the perception and constitution of democracy and surrounding discursive element in the text corpus. Each section begins with a collection of quotes which is thought to serve as an illustration. The discussion of each the statement follows along the lines of the four analytical dimensions or statement functions.

3.2.1 *Competitive Electoral Systems and Preference Aggregation*

"The main features of democracy [are]: 1. institutionally established procedures that regulate, 2. competition for control over political authority 3. on the basis of deliberation, 4. where nearly all adult citizens are permitted to participate in 5. an electoral mechanism where their expressed preferences over alternative candidates determine the outcome, 6. in such ways that the government is responsive to the majority or to as many as possible." (JCMS 2006: 547)

"[...] contestation for political leadership and argument over the direction of the policy agenda is ultimately the difference between a democracy and an enlightened form of benevolent authoritarianism." (JCMS 2006: 534).

"Democracy as Ideal (a1a): Tell us, please, what do you think about the idea that a democracy, in which multiple parties compete for power, is the best system for governing [the country]?" (JCMS 2010: 1101).

"For Schattschneider (1960, p. 141), modern democracy is 'a competitive political system in which competing leaders and organizations define the alternatives of public policy in such a way that the public can participate in the decision-making process'. And for Brian Barry (1991, pp. 24–61), a democratic procedure is 'a method of determining the content of laws (and other legally binding decisions) such that the preferences of the citizens have some formal connection with the outcome in which each counts equally [and] allow for the formulation, expression, and aggregation of political preferences'." (JCMS 2006: 547)

"[The Treaty of the EU] establishes a dual basis of democratic legitimacy: the representation of citizens in the EP (Article 10(2), first paragraph TEU) and the representation of Member States in the Council and in the European Council, which are democratically accountable to their national parliaments or to their citizens (Article 10(2), second paragraph TEU). In order for citizens and national parliamentarians to hold the politicians in the Council and European Council accountable, they must be able to attribute responsibility for decisions to their particular government." (JCMS 2014: 687)

"The increased transparency and powers of the European Parliament and national parliaments may foster political contestation. This is not to deny that transparency also may carry costs regarding the quality and efficiency of agreements, for instance by foreclosing the creative exploration of new options (Elster, 1998, p. 98; Naurin, 2004). This loss of efficiency in individual cases does not outweigh the benefits of political contestation and more trustworthy institutions." (JCMS 2006: 555)

The equation between democracy and political representation, general elections and party pluralism – in short with "competitive electoral system[s]" (JCMS 2004: 984) – that was cited in the secondary literature does indeed seem to be at play in the text corpus as an underlying assumption about what democracy entails, which informs otherwise diverging sentences and positions. Connections between the terms are frequent, both in implicit and explicit form (cf. for instance JCMS 2006: 45; JCMS 2007: 58; JCMS 2009: 20; JCMS 2014: 337, 687). To illustrate, one of the text passages cited above measures "attitudes towards democracy" by asking a sample of respondents for their thoughts about "the idea that a democracy, in which multiple parties compete for power, is the best system" of government (JCMS 2010: 1101). In another passage, "contestation for political leadership" is described as the ultimate "difference between a democracy and an enlightened form of benevolent authoritarianism" (JCMS 2006: 534). Yet other text passages defines the core elements of democracy as "procedures" that regulate:

"competition for control over political authority [in] an electoral mechanism where [citizen-]expressed preferences over alternative candidates determine the outcome" (JCMS 2006: 547)

Crucially, "critical" accounts, including such that draw on normative arguments and knowledge from law and philosophy, overarchingly attempt to extend, deepen or add further elements to this conception – for instance, by emphasizing "the need for a public space in which people with diverse views exchange opinions to arrive at a common understanding and policies" (JCMS 2008: 471; cf. also JCMS 2006: 550). However, other than in the form of additions, challenges to the equation "democracy = representation + party competition + general elections" as such do *not* occur. Thus, in Foucauldian terms, I believe that subversions to this equation can be understood as a "lack" or "unsaid"; a silence that delineates the borders of the reasonably "speakable" in the text material (Foucault [1970] 2010: 210; on the concept of the "unsaid", cf. also Carter 2006).

Now, how are these "core" democratic elements related and ordered? What is seen to constitute the "glue" between them? In the texts, mechanisms of representation, election and competition are frequently understood to serve the purpose of producing a "match" between "public" or "citizen preferences" and "policy outcomes". For instance, it is argued that the EU suffers from a "democratic deficit" since "EU citizens' preferences on issues on the EU policy agenda at best have only an indirect influence on EU policy outcomes" (JCMS 2006: 573). "Competition" between political parties and/or candidates by means of general elections is seen to ensure the "accountability of political leaders", thereby making them "responsive to the best interests of voters" and thus distinguishable from "benevolent but non-accountable rulers" who lack "institutionalized mechanisms that make them trustworthy" (JCMS 2006: 545). Accountability, therefore, is perceived as a consequence of competition – if voters are not satisfied, they can de-elect representatives, thereby "holding them accountable". The term "transparency" instead functions as a condition or technique for enhancing and improving competition for voter satisfaction by ensuring that citizens have sufficient information to "monitor the performance of their delegated representatives" (2008: 108); or, in an alternative wording, to "determine whether leaders could have done better" and "identify who is responsible for policies" (JCMS 2006: 548). Against this background, a statement can formulated:

Statement 1

In democratic political systems, competition between parties and/or candidates for power by means of free and fair general elections serves to ensure that leaders are accountable and policy output corresponds with citizens' policy preferences. Transparency and openness help improve this mechanism by increasing the amount and correctness of information available to voters about what party/leader is responsible for what policy.

What epistemic, discursive conditions are necessary for such a statement to emerge? How can one describe its "referential" in the sense of "laws of possibility, rules of existence for the objects and relations" (Foucault [1970] 2010: 91) which it names, establishes or denies? To start with, the underlying perception of "democratic" politics as a sum of individual preferences and mechanisms for their aggregation implies an understanding of the individual (preference holder) as the origin, the actual source of political demands and wishes. Rather than economic classes, religious groups, social movements or any other imaginable political subject, the individual citizen is assumed to be the relevant, primary subject of politics. Accordingly, lacking correspondence between preferences and policy "output" is attributed to deficits in the institutional structure or to information problems which find their solution in increased transparency and openness, rather than to, for instance, any kind of conflict between elites and subordinate groups about beliefs or resources. The citizenry, perceived of as a sum or aggregate, hence becomes the only thinkable, relevant collective. A further "rule of existence" (Foucault [1970] 2010: 91) can be identified in the exclusion inherent to the terms "citizen" and "citizenry" of all those unable to fully claim this title: children, foreigners, the mad or insane and possibly the criminal.

The equation between politics and the political system which was touched upon earlier (cf. above 3.13) fulfills a stabilizing function and provides certainty about the boundaries of the statement by delineating the sphere of the mandate and kind of power which is competed for in democratic elections: the legally regulated control over *political institutions*. Finally, the statement implies an equation between representation and democracy. It does so by implicitly establishing the question of whose preferences influence policy outcomes as the criteria distinguishing between democracy and, say, oligarchy, polyarchy, etc., rather than the question of who is governing and exerting power in a more direct sense. In this respect, a certain similarity can therefore be identified to the logics and discursive equations in US discourses on democracy (promotion) and foreign policy as described by Robinson (1996, 2013) and Burron (2011, 2012).

With regard to the associated domain, the statement inscribes itself in discourses on political systems and institutions in political science and legal and political philosophy, but it also draws on perceptions associated with economics and statistics in conceiving of the democratic political process as a question of aggregation and competition. The access to and command of these domains of knowledge determine the subject position that anyone would have to occupy in order to reproduce the statement; in order to "be its subject". The subject position therefore strongly resembles the position of the "social scientist" that was mentioned in the earlier discussion of the enunciative modalities (cf. above 3.14), although it draws more specifically on descriptive, analytical traditions and processes of knowledge production. The repeatable materiality that allows for the statement to be reproduced, on the one hand, is made up of social-science institutions, universities, text production and so forth. On the other hand, the statement also inscribes itself in the material or sense-perceptible reality through the existence of the very institutions it is "making sense of": the elections, representation in parliaments, political parties.

3.2.2 *Power Constraints, Scrutiny and the Balancing of Forces*

> "We see a policy process as contributing to the quality of democracy when it takes place according to established formal procedures [...] Furthermore, based on existing literature on state capture, we stress the link between the adherence to proper (formal) procedures in the policy process (rule of law) and limiting state capture and corruption." (JCMS 2014: 140)

> "The EU's institutional structures protect democratic legitimacy by preventing abuses of power by the people. The very multiplicity of authorities and interests engaged in the elaborate EU interest consultation process ensures a kind of mutual horizontal control." (JCMS 2004: 985)

> "Indicators Democratic Legitimacy: - Parliamentary scrutiny (investigation rights, active consultation) - Ministers are accountable to parliament - Parliament approves appointments - Parliament controls policy plans and budgets." (JCMS 2008: 109)

> "[...] while provisions for the open pursuit of political conflict are

> a necessary and defining feature of every democratic system, in highly fragmented polities conflict more easily risks degenerating into damaging degrees of intense polarization. Such systems must thus structurally facilitate the clash of competing political interests while at the same time mitigating the danger posed by its most acrimonious and extreme potential mani-festations." (JCMS 2012: 793)

> "Without formally violating the rule of law, [political developments in Hungary and Romania since 2010] contravene basic principles of liberal democratic competition and fundamental freedoms. The [Hungarian] government has concentrated and entrenched its power. It weakened notably the constitutional court, seized control of key public institutions (by packing them with party loyalists and extending mandates much beyond the term of parliament), changed the electoral law and requires two-thirds majorities to change some of its policies. In Romania, [...] the new government suspended the centre-right president, Traian Basescu. Through emergency ordinances it removed constitutional checks on the impeachment procedure, including a weakening of the constitutional court and a lifting of the 50 per cent participation quorum for the referendum required to validate the impeachment." (JCMS 2014: 106)

While the main assumptions inherent to the constitution of democracy as a set of institutions and procedures aiming to engender a convergence between citizen preferences and policy outcomes remain unchallenged throughout the text corpus, the picture is slightly complicated by the presence of further conditions that seem to delineate what "truly" counts as a democratic political process and polity. In particular, a series of constraints on the power of political "leaders" and institutions reappear throughout the texts, which go beyond the criteria that power over political institutions ought to be obtained through free and fair general elections and exercised through a time-constrained mandate. Instead, a series of objects circulate in the texts that pertain to the processes of governing nd the modalities of power exertion and are constituted as necessary to spread and divide political power amongst actors and institutions, thereby creating a "balance", "equilibrium" or "reconciliation" between societal forces and, at the same time, precluding the eruption of harmful conflictuality (JCMS 2010: 745; JCMS 2012: 192, 794). These limitations include respect for individual and minority rights by political mandate holders, but also processes of mutual scrutiny between political institutions in the form of "parliamentary control of the executive" or the "separation of powers" and the scrutiny of leaders and institutions by "independent civil society" actors, the "free media" and interest-group/civil-society consultation procedures (JCMS 2005: 33, 165; JCMS 2008: 15, 108, 156; JCMS 2009: 691; JCMS 2010: 745; JCMS 2012: 793; JCMS 2014: 106, 140). For instance, one paragraph lists parliamentary scrutiny, the accountability of ministers to parliament, parliamentary controls, policy plans and budgets as indicators that can be used to measure the democratic legitimacy of a given polity (JCMS 2008: 109), while another asserts that "interest consultation processes" contribute to the same aim (JCMS 2004: 945). Yet others parenthetically state that "concentration of media power" in Italy amounts to a breach of "democratic principles" (JCMS 2010: 794) or criticize that "the EU has turned a blind eye to the increasingly autocratic governing style of Yanukovych, including the pressures on the opposition and civil society and the free media" (JCMS 2012: 379). Furthermore, legal limitations also figure prominently in this context. Discursive objects such as the "rule of law", "constitutional rules", "checks" and "constraints" or the "independence of courts" are understood to limit the power of political power holders so as to enhance "democratic legitimacy" and prevent individual institutions from "concentrat[ing] and entrench[ing] power" (JCMS 2014: 106). In the text corpus, democratic governance is therefore constituted as contingent on a range of institutional and legal safeguards against the dangers of "anti-democratic and unaccountable concentration of power" and "harmful polarization" between social, political groups (JCMS 2012: 102; cf. also JCMS 2012: 140; JCMS 2014: 106). In other words, democracy is seen to necessitate procedures for creating a peaceful balance between a plurality of societal forces and limiting state/political power. Against this background, a second statement can be defined as follows:

Statement 2

In order to avoid harmful centralization and abuse of power, democratic governance requires a set of legal and institutional constraints that engender a peaceful balance between societal forces: the subjection of political mandate holders to the rule of law, the contingency of policy on the respect for individual and minority rights, the separation of powers between political institutions, procedures for mutual scrutiny and control between such institutions, as well as scrutiny of state power by independent civil society actors and a free media.

Again, in describing the statement, let us first turn to a discussion of its "referential" (Foucault [1970] 2010: 91). A central condition for such a statement to emerge as an underlying delineation of what can (reasonably) be said about "democracy" seems to me to be an implicit anxiety, or assumption about polarization, turbulence and violence as dangers inherent to political relations and processes, and the associated perception that such conflictuality ought to be channelled and made manageable by means of the said constraints and institutions. As I mentioned briefly in the description of the rules of formation, "balance", "peace" and "stability" are closely connected with democracy through out the text corpus, while "violence", "instability", "turbulence" and so on are generally put in opposition to the term. For instance, a sentence concerned with the 2004 eastern enlargement of the Union maintains that:

"while the new member states [had mastered] a rapid and radical transformation in order to consolidate democracy and 'return to Europe' their domestic political systems still showed signs of instability" (JCMS 2005: 163).

Another article formulates the following hypothesis about EU democracy promotion:

"*H5b:* If there is latent or open instability in a country, the EU will commit itself to even more support in order to increase stability" (JCMS 2011: 1002).

Support for democracy is equated with support for stability. The concern with power centralization and the perceived containment of this danger through the subjection of power holders to the rule of law, the separation of powers between political institutions, processes of scrutiny, critique by society actors and so forth, furthermore, seems to presuppose an specific understanding of power and consequently also of its abuse, as being attributable mainly to the state apparatus. Here, the separations between the economy and the political, state and society, public and private (cf. above 3.13) once again function as stabilizing regularities making political (not economic), public (not private) domination exerted by the state (not by societal actors) towards society the stuff of concern: the decisive criteria for determining whether or not a society is democratic. That is, patterns of domination in working conditions or domination resulting from an uneven distribution of economic resources, inequality in sexual relations, reproduction or any other kind of power relations might be deemed detrimental to democracy by some, but they are not directly relevant for determining if a society or a state is democratic.

Similar to the first statement, the associated domain that makes it possible for the statement to be conceived of as an intelligible part of "a particular context" (Foucault [1970] 2010: 98) can be identified in social-science knowledge production about the art of government, in this case in particular as regarding the law and the workings of political institutions. Accordingly, the subject position can be described as an intersection between that of the legal scholar, the law professional, the educated (EU or national) bureaucrat or the political scientist engaging in the field of inquiry that is usually termed "the study of political systems" when research areas within the discipline are juxtaposed and ordered. The statement's repeatable materiality encompasses both the sphere of scientific re-articulation, the repetition of theories and knowledge production through text, talk and academic institutions, but also the institutions described in the statement: the "democratic" state apparatus, procedures of control, separation of mandates, civil society organizations and so forth.

3.2.3 *Deliberation, Identity and Trust in Elites*

> "[Without] policy debates including deliberation concerning the best means and objectives of policies [...] voters would not be able to form their preferences on complex policy issues." (JCMS 2006: 550)
>
> "there is broad agreement between democratic theorists that the citizens' preferences that do matter are those that have a chance of being created or modified within arenas of political contestation, and that what matters are institutions that reliably ensure that policies are responsive to these preferences, rather than matching by happy coincidence." (JCMS 2006: 556)

“A key difference between standard democratic and non-democratic regimes, however, is that citizens form their views about which policy options they prefer through the processes of deliberation and party contestation that are essential elements of all democracies.” (JCMS 2006: 545)

“The minimalist definition [of democracy] refers to an electoral-based approach pertaining to the competitive struggle for people’s votes, the maximalist definition (Held, 1996) embraces the normative underpinnings of democracy and underlines the importance of participation, citizenship and participatory democracy (Lappin, 2010, p. 193).” (JCMS 2012: 370)

“[the quality of the democratic process] ultimately depends on citizens being willing and able to follow and engage in democratic debate and deliberation, to vote and, most crucially, to accept the possibility of being outvoted by a majority from other Member States without rejecting the legitimacy of the [...] democratic process itself.” (JCMS 2012: 785)

“[...] voter dissatisfaction leads to rapid cycling of governments, especially in the central and east European countries (CEECs); and electoral radicalization. Some citizens have moved far to the right – blaming EU-sanctioned immigration for unemployment and EU institutions for the loss of national sovereignty and identity. Others have moved far to the left – blaming off-shoring to Asia, ‘near-shoring’ to eastern Europe and liberalizing EU institutions for challenges to long-standing labour institutions and the welfare state. Yet others have turned to interest group politics, joined social movements and supported INGOs in actively trying to make a difference.” (JCMS 2009: 22)

“Citizens with more extreme political orientations are less supportive of democracy. Political extremism in general is related to political ideologies that do not tolerate political pluralism, competition and opposition. This holds for right-wing extremism [...] and – perhaps to a smaller extent – for those on the far left of the political spectrum [...]. Right-wing as well as left-wing political extremists also tend to be more disposed to censor and suppress their political opponents [...] – orientations that are in-

> compatible with democratic principles." (JCMS 2014: 865)
>
> "Given that 'populism' may be defined as the presentation of society as divided between the blameless 'us' against whom injustices are carried out and the harmful 'others' who carry out these injustices, we may understand it as a blame-shifting mechanism grounded on a rhetoric of exclusivity vis-à-vis other groups. [...] This entails an engagement in a populist blame-shifting game – that is, a focus on who is to blame for the crisis, directing responsibility to a range of 'others'. Therefore we should expect that: *H3*: Populist rhetoric is likely to be expressed in the forms of blame-shifting and exclusivity. Populist rhetoric does vary, however, in its presentation of which groups may be seen as the dominant/privileged ones and which elites should be excluded." (JCMS 2014: 392)
>
> "Eder ably backs up this thesis with an essay on populism that alludes to parallels with Latin America. She claims that representative institutions and legislatures are weakened when peasants and the urban masses are integrated through top-down mobilization and anti-establishment discourse." (2004: 431)

In addition to the regularities we have so far discussed, a further category of sentences in the text corpus imply and bring forth limits regarding the spectrum of political positions or preferences that ought – and ought *not* – to be included in the democratic political processes. Just like the second statement, which we just discussed, this textual regularity does not challenge the perception of democracy as a procedure for citizen preference aggregation through competition, as was described in the first statement. Instead, it imposes additional limits as to what really counts as democratic, hence adding to the specificity of the discursive constitution of the term. To put it simply, while the core elements of democracy are overarchingly understood in the way that the first statement describes, not all "citizen preferences" are seen as worthy of inclusion into the aggregation exercise. In particular, the frequent occurrence of oppositions contrasting "democracy" with "extremism", "populism", and sometimes "ideology", "fundamentalism" or "Islamism" point to a general exclusion of positions that are perceived of as less "rational", "educated" or "responsible" and thus as threatening the stability and trust in political institutions and elites (cf. JCMS 2004: 1667; JCMS 2006: 534; JCMS 2008: 5, 691, 912; JCMS 2009: 691; JCMS 2010: 749; JCMS 2012: 379, 589, 793; JCMS 2014: 105, 861, 866). The term "populism" is associated with "blame-shifting" rhetoric, antagonistic critiques of elites and weakening of representative institutions; As a consequence it is understood to constitute "irresponsible" political behavior and as exploiting irrational, uneducated popular opinion (JCMS 2004: 431, JCMS 2013: 338, JCMS 2014: 388, 392). Extremism instead subsumes any political position, "left" or "right", perceived to be too "far away" from the imagined political "middle" of contemporary arrangements and beliefs (cf. above 3.11). The term "extremism" hence borders on "radicalism", is associated with violence and irrationality, ideology, terrorism and, like populism, with "blaming others" rather than being responsible and active (inter alia 2008: 118; 2013: 146; 2014: 866). While the ordered participation on the part of citizens in established political procedures (referenda, elections and civil society) is perceived to increase the "quality" of democracy, "abstentionism", "low turn-outs", "cynicism about elites" or "anti-establishment discourse" are seen as the product or seed of "extremism" (JCMS 2004: 431, 990, 911; JCMS 2007: 747; JCMS 2009: 20; JCMS 2010: 655; JCMS 2011: 655; JCMS 2012: 793). For instance, responsible citizens who are "actively trying to make a difference" by joining NGOs and civil society movements, are contrasted with "radicalization", "blaming" others, acting out of "dissatisfaction" and provoking "rapid cycling of governments" (JCMS 2009: 22). Once again, the discursive representation of "democracy" in the text corpus thus locates the term in close proximity to political stability and the acceptance and affirmation of established governance structures and elites, while positions that are deemed to be "extremist and "populist" are excluded from the realm of acceptable preferences and reasonable speech.

Now, do the texts offer any remedy for the described socio-political maladies? Indeed, a series of objects including "public deliberation", "dialogue", a "dynamic public sphere" and "communicative discourse" figure as ways of improving and rationalization citizen preferences, thus "legitimizing" policy and strengthening the "quality of democracy" (JCMS 2004: 993-4; JCMS 2006: 545, 550; JCMS 2008: 455; JCMS 2010: 906; JCMS 2012: 786, 792; JCMS 2013: 340). As one articulation postulates, "the citizens' preferences that do matter are those that have a chance of being created or modified" (JCMS 2006: 556) in such arenas. Moreover, citizen participation in public debates and deliberation is perceived of as helping to "instill a sense of public ownership", as strengthening the "trust" of the general public in "political elites" and thus as fulfilling a function in containing the spread of populism/extremism (JCMS 2004: 992; JCMS 2006: 545, 560; JCMS 2012: 367, 789). Conversely, any "absence of substantive discourse and deliberation" risks being "exploited by the extremes on both sides of the political spectrum" (JCMS 2004: 990).

Besides communication, dialogue and deliberation, a strong "sense of community", "collective identity", "demos" and "communal identification" also figure as sources of trust in elites and institutions, and conditions for high-quality, stable democracy: "Democratic decision-making demands non-instrumental commitments and [...] these require shared communal identifications" (JCMS 2012: 787). In the EU member states, communal identifications, collective identities and so forth are generally perceived to stem from a certain degree of homogeneity among citizens in terms of culture, language and history or "shared historical memory" (JCMS 2004: 976-9; JCMS 2009: 683; JCMS 2012: 790, 794). Conversely, the perceived comparative *lack* of such homogeneity in the EU as a whole is the object of a fierce scholarly search throughout the text corpus for alternative sources of collective identification in order to remedy the resulting "democratic deficit" of the EU (JCMS 2009: 683; JCMS 2012: 783; JCMS 2013: 336, 356). Collective identity, communal identification or a sense of belonging to a demos therefore appear as sources of commitment to participate in official political processes, of willingness to submit to their outcomes and as "solutions" to the interconnected dangers of "populism", "extremism", "abstentionism" or "lack of trust". Conversely, the "quality" of democracy is perceived of as contingent on:

"citizens being willing and able to follow and engage in democratic debate and deliberation, to vote and, most crucially, to accept the possibility of being outvoted." (JCMS 2012: 785)

Taken together, an underlying textual regularity can be identified that connects the maturation or formation of citizen preferences and participation in established procedures through dialogue, collective identity and participation with stability and trust in elites, hence delineating the borders separating democracy from populism and extremism. As a statement,

I believe it might be formulated as follows:

Statement 3

In advanced, high-quality democracies, public deliberation and strong collective identities strengthen the legitimacy of governance and function as safeguards against populism and extremism: public deliberation and dialogue help render citizens' policy preferences and political opinions more rational, educated, responsible and moderate, while collective identification strengthens citizens' trust in political elites and institutions, their willingness to participate in debates, elections and referenda and to submit themselves to the outcomes of established political procedures.

How can we describe the statement's referential in the sense of its laws of possibility or the discursive conditions for its emergence (Foucault [1970] 2010: 91)? One requirement for the emergence of the above statement seems to be a perception that dialogue, deliberation or linguistic interaction bears the potential of fostering an approximation to a rational consensus—to educate and enlighten its participants. That is, speech can be stripped of power so as to amount to a kind of communicative interaction that posses an inherent, inclusive rationality: the possibility of a "public space in which people with diverse views exchange opinions to arrive at a common understanding and policies" (JCMS 2008: 455). A necessary condition for such a perception, in turn, can be identified in the oppositions between reason and madness, truth and falsity. Moreover, the border between democracy and populism seems to rest upon and draw certainty from the opposition between rationality and affection, responsibility and opportunism/blame-shifting.

The recurring notion that collective identification strengthens trust in elites instead rests on the implicit assumption that the relevant collective encompasses both "elites" and subjects who do not belong to this category. Hence, the relevant collective is neither a social or economic class, nor any other subordinate group without (theoretical) access to positions within the "elite". Instead, the notion that democracy derives from the subject of a "citizenry", a "demos" or a "people" once again seems to be at play here. As discussed with regard to the first statement, such conceptions establish boundaries for who is to be included and excluded in the processes that the statement names and describes – with foreigners, children, mentally ill, etc., being deemed irrelevant for the legitimacy of political representation, participation in deliberation and so on. Depending on what is seen to unite the "people" besides the legal title of citizenship or to constitute the glue of "collective identifications", categories such as language, culture, norms and/or history also constitute latent sources of exclusion.

In terms of the associated domain, the statement inscribes itself in normative political philosophy, knowledge about ethics and legitimacy. In particular, Habermasian discourse ethics and deliberative theories of democracy in general constitute a powerful part of the associated domain by providing certainty about the representative content of articulations asserting or assuming logical connections between communicative interaction and enlightenment or reason. Moreover, the statement also draws certainty from sociology and the study of collective identities, instrumental and non-instrumental commitments and patterns of social behavior. Accordingly, the subject position is that of the social science scholar mastering the said domains. However, articulations revolving around the rationality of communicative processes also seem to me to draw on a position of a "neutral" subject that resembles the Rawlsian "veil of ignorance" (cf. above 3.12) in so far that the absence of any position in society, and thus of "bias" or "interest", is the defining criteria that makes possible true speech about normative concerns.

The repeatable materiality resembles that of the earlier statements; on the one hand, the statement is reproduced through texts, institutions and speech within the philosophy and social science academy. On the other hand, it might also be reproduced and hence attain a material form in determining the shape of political institutions, programs and governance practices.

3.2.4 *The International Spread of Democracy: Hierarchy and Advancement*

> "The state of democracy [in ENP countries] is worlds apart. Vachudova (2005) has argued that a condition for the enlargement policy's success in the recent candidate countries has been the presence of political competition, and the EU's ability to stimulate this competition. However, while the average polity/demo-

cracy score for the candidate states in 1993 was 8.36, the 2003 average score for the ENP countries is –1.00 and the standard deviation is large. Thus, the neighbourhood countries differ considerably from the 1993 candidate countries in their stage of maturity towards the values the EU seeks to promote." (JCMS 2006: 44)

"Commissioner Vitorino is right when he stresses that the EU and the US have a key common objective. It should be expressed more explicitly that the nature of the common objective cannot be security for its own sake, but security to protect the western values of freedom, democracy and the rule of law." (JCMS 2004: 1078)

"The achievement of peace, stability, political moderation and protection of human rights in a region that had experienced wars, nationalist divisions, Nazism and Fascism, is a transformation from which the EU can derive justifiable satisfaction. Since the early 1990s the EU has been striving to export its successful model of peace through democracy and of democratization through trade (Nicolaïdis and Howse, 2002, p. 768) to other parts of the world, thereby extending its sphere of economic and normative influence." (JCMS 2010: 582)

"The concept of 'Normative Power' refers to the ability to exert 'power over opinion' (Manners, 2002, p. 239). It pertains, in the European internal context, to the EU's ability to ground its integration agenda in a distinctive normative foundation (peace through economic integration and the pursuance of democracy, human rights, environmental protection, etc.). Externally, this concept relates to the EU's attempts to export that normative 'European Model' elsewhere. In the words of Manners, "Normative Power Europe embodies 'an attempt to suggest that not only is the EU constructed on a normative basis, but more importantly that this predisposes it to act in a normative way in world politics' (Manners, 2002, p. 252)." (JCMS 2010: 582)

"In terms of top-down democracy promotion, the AP [Action Plan] puts very clear demands on Ukraine's compliance with electoral standards. It requires democratic presidential and parliamentary elections in Ukraine in accordance with OSCE standards, gradual approximation of Ukraine legislation, norms and standards with those of the EU, the independence of the judiciary and development of administrative capacities." (JCMS 2010: 1219)

"Although the Mexican government at the time still did not fully accept the involvement of NGOs in making such decisions, it slowly began to realize that a healthy civil society was a hallmark of 'first world' democracies." (JCMS 2005: 185)

"Despite the danger of backsliding that the changing incentive structure after accession evokes, studies initially suggested that the EU's new Member States have experienced at best a slowdown, rather than a reversal, of preaccession democratic and good governance reforms (Levitz and Pop-Eleches, 2010; Pridham, 2008; Sedelmeier, 2012; Spendzharova and Vachudova, 2012)." (JCMS 2014: 105-6)

"Ensuring the sustainable implementation of democratic reforms in third countries is a challenge for foreign policy and for international activity at large. Since the Arab Spring, the EU has been criticized for the insufficiency and ineffectiveness of its external democracy promotion, for its inability to convince reluctant regimes to consider political reform as an objective for cooperation, and for its failure to improve its instruments and incentives towards reform-willing partners. This edited volume assesses the implementation of European democracy promotion on the ground, asking how the EU and its Member States promote democratic developments in key states (Morocco, Ukraine, Nigeria and Iraq) and strategically important regions (Balkans, Central Asia and Gulf)." (JCMS 2013, 371)

"[Democracy promotion] instruments can be differentiated along many lines: bottom-up vs top-down, state- vs civil-society-oriented (Carothers, 1999; Diamond, 1999, p. 218), bilateral vs multilateral (Pevehouse, 2005), instruments that respect sovereignty vs intrusive instruments, and strong or weak instruments. Most often, instruments are classified along the positive–negative dimension (Burnell, 2000, p. 6; Hazelzet, 2001): the strategy is to

> reward positive developments, i.e. towards a liberal democracy, using 'positive' measures, and to punish negative developments using 'negative' measures. Existing alternative and more elaborate classifications are, in our view, supplementary rather than complementary. For instance, a favorable declaration issued by the Presidency of the EU on the occasion of a 'fair' election is a bilateral, weak, non-intrusive, top-down and rewarding (and thus positive) instrument." (JCMS 2011: 999)

The final set of textual regularities in the JCMS text corpus that I would like to discuss links our analysis to the international realm and the perception of EU external governance techniques as reflecting a commitment to the international spread of "democracy". In the text corpus, sentences concerned with EU external relations and the Union's role in international affairs are characterized by underlying assumptions about the normative desirability of EU and/or Western democracy promotion programs, of a "normative", "ethical" nature of EU foreign policy and about "democracy" as constituting a European, or Western value (JCMS 2004: 1665; JCMS 2005: 189; JCMS 2006: 42; JCMS 2010: 582; JCMS 2005: 189; JCMS 2007: 515, 517; JCMS 2010: 582; JCMS 2011: 997). Inter alia, scholarly investigations frequently start "from the premise that the European Union and the United States 'are united by a normative commitment to democracy" (JCMS 2011: 490). Or, in an alternative wording "at the most basic level, assume that the EU is motivated to engage as a 'democracy promoter'" (JCMS 2010: 593).

Crucially, self-acclaimed critical accounts question neither the desirability or principle feasibility of democracy promotion, nor the perception of democracy as constituting a value, norm or principle of European origin or quality. Instead, critical examinations of EU governance techniques are overarchingly concerned with lacking results of EU governance techniques aiming to promote the "spread" of democracy from the EU to other territories, thus proposing how to improve pro-grams, how to make EU influence more effective or decrying any perceived prioritization of other "foreign policy objectives" such as, for instance, counterterrorism at the expense of democracy promotion (JCMS 2008: 16, 147; JCMS 2009: 691; JCMS 2013: 371). In other words, the main concerns of scholars are the efficiency of governance techniques, conditions for improving and strengthening their assumed effects, explaining the variation in EU “commitments” between different countries, regions, etc., and to identifying causal explanation for the distribution of funds and intervention programs. That is, with investigating different aspects of “the EU as an actor in democracy [...] ‘export’“ (JCMS 2013: 370; cf. also JCMS 2009: 691; JCMS 2011: 1002; JCMS 2013: 371; JCMS 2014: 106).

This textual pattern, in turn, is supported by the variety of hierarchical identity descriptions that I touched upon earlier (cf. 3.12). That is, the perception that democracy is something European, or Western, and that the EU should “export” it to other regions, is stabilized and made more certain against the backdrop of binary identity descriptions contrasting the “EU”, “Europe”, “the West”, “first world democracies”, “substantive democracies”, “higher-quality democracies” or “developed industrial democracies” with categories such as “transitional countries”, “target countries”, “post-communist systems”, “hybrid regimes”, “emerging democracies”, “grey-zone democracies” or “reluctant democratizers”, “authoritarian regimes”, “autocracy”, etc. (JCMS 2005: 185, 190; JCMS 2007: 521, 526; JCMS 2008: 20; JCMS 2009: 691). As noted earlier, such hierarchizations are underlined by the occurrence of grading systems that measure the “quality” or “level” of democracy (JCMS 2004: 213; JCMS 2006: 44; JCMS 2010: 743), but also by recurring equations of terms such as “development” or “progress” with assimilation to Western/EU values and political arrangements: “the approximation of [...] legislation, norms and standards with those of the EU” (JCMS 2010: 1219; cf. also JCMS 2004: 223; JCMS 2007: 526; JCMS 2010: 1209). Moreover, in sentences forming around the concept of “eastern enlargement”, the opposition between democracy and communism is particularly frequent and functions as a boundary that allows for and stabilizes an equation between democratization, EU accession and transition to market economy, which are understood as interconnected processes of societal progress (JCMS 2004: 213; JCMS 2010: 1086, 1092). The same pattern is observable in the context of the southern enlargement round, which is described as a process of “economic liberalization and democratic consolidation” (JCMS 2004: 221; cf. also JCMS 2006: 663). With a view to both EU enlargement rounds and foreign policy towards more distant regions, one can thus discern a logic that equates the Union's influence with democratization and societal advancement in the sense of a normatively desirable and logically interconnected combination of peace, domestic stability, political moderation, “a flourishing market economy” and a “vibrant civil society” (cf. JCMS 2006: 44, 665; JCMS 2007: 48, 58; JCMS 2008: 20, 901; JCMS 2009: 20, 919; JCMS 2010: 740; JCMS 2011: 997, 1002; JCMS 2012: 519, 589, 618). To a certain extent this regularity echoes Hobson's findings that narratives about liberal democracy as a universal, normatively superior form of government that progressively spreads around the globe constitute dominant contemporary perceptions in international affairs and IR research (2009: 634-7, cf. above 1.2).

How then is such change thought to come about? A set of analytical classifications recurs throughout the texts which serves to order and differentiate between “logics of influence” (2011: 490) that are perceived to emanate from democracy promotion governance techniques. For instance, “bottom up” instruments are understood as changing society from “below” by empowering “pro-democratic” civil society, which in turn “pressures” government institutions to engage in “reforms”, while “top-down” instruments instead aim at changing the “incentive structure” of target country governments by employing “conditionality” techniques – that is, by punishing and/or rewarding behavioral choices by policy makers (cf. inter alia JCMS 2004: 985; JCMS 2007: 62; JCMS 2009: 20; JCMS 2010: 1218; JCMS 2011: 999; JCMS 2012: 370). Further categories aiming to describe and explain the Union's “influence” include “normative suasion”, “capacity-building” directed at political institutions and “socialization” of political elites so as to internalize “EU values” (JCMS 2011: 490, 999). Notably, the EU is understood to exert “soft”, “civilian” forms of power; to exert “‘power over opinion’” (JCMS 2010: 582) rather than by coercion and to do so out of normative concerns rather than material or self-interest:

“[the EU] has become influential by promoting values, policies and goals that appeal to other states in a way that aggression and coercion cannot” (JCMS 2007: 520; cf. also JCMS 2010: 593).

Taken together, we can thus define an discursive regularity that places the EU at an advanced stage of societal development and a resulting perception that the EU engages in ethical, normatively desirable behavior when trying to export its normative standards and social-economical arrangements to less developed societies by soft, civilian foreign policy techniques.

Statement 4

EU external relations policies can and should provoke progressive societal change in other countries and regions towards stable, moderate, free and peaceful democratic political systems and economic prosperity through free-market economy. As an advanced entity, the EU promotes such advancement towards its own level of political and economic development primarily in non-violent ways: by setting negative and/or positive incentives for reforms, by socializing and convincing elites and empowering democratic civil society actors who engage in critiques of undemocratic governance.

As with the earlier statements, let us begin by discussing what might be considered to constitute the statement's referential. The perceptions summarized in the statement imply a specific notion of societal, historical development as a progression along hierarchically ordered "stages" of civilization. That is, different societies might find themselves at different steps on this latter and they might progress with different speed or even experience periods of "backsliding" (JCMS 2014: 105), but they cannot "make progress" in different directions. The statement thus implies a perception of history that draws on notions of advancement and improvement, while placing the EU and the West at the forefront thereof. This implicit understanding stabilizes the perception of EU external relations governance techniques and foreign policy more generally, as something "ethical" or "normative" since the EU can be seen to *help* others advance towards its own level of development – to enhance "their stage of maturity towards the values the EU seeks to promote" (JCMS 2006: 44), to progress towards becoming a "full member of the group of 'first world' democracies" (JCMS 2005: 185) and so forth.

As a further discursive condition of existence, the above fourth statement also seems to me to rely on a specific way of imagining societal change and of situating the societal locus of power. While violent, coercive methods are perceived of as being precluded by, or less appropriate considering, the EU's "civilian", "ethical, "normative" identity, change is provoked by "convincing" elites through dialogue and socialization, by changing beliefs, creating international pressure from civil society or setting (material) incentives for elites to act in certain ways. This echoes a notion of power as repressive and violent rather than productive. Moreover, despite the frequent occurrence of sentences referring to the "empowerment" of civil society, power is once again attributed mainly to the sovereign state apparatus, with independent civil society functioning as a check aiming to restrict this principle source of domination.

Finally, the boundaries defining the perception of what characterizes a "high-quality", "first-world" or "advanced" democracy are instead defined by the discursive regularities discussed so far: representation, party pluralism/opposition, free and fair elections, accountability, openness, a strong civil society and free media, limitations and separation of powers, stability, inclusion of citizens in established non-violent moderate forms of participation and submission to the outcomes of such procedures are all echoed in descriptions of governance programs, in policy advice on how to improve them and so on. The following paragraph deploring the lacking success of EU democracy promotion efforts in Northern Africa illustrates the structuring effects of these regularities:

"In Egypt, President Mubarak has largely ruled by emergency law, has obstructed opposition forces, banned Muslim organizations and restricted NGO activity. Neither the 2000 nor 2005 elections were free and fair. Syria is notoriously non-democratic and, in spite of Libya's recent opening to the west, it still lacks political parties. The liberalization in Algeria in the mid-1990s failed to produce meaningful improvements, Islamist opposition is banned, and civil society activity is minimal." (JCMS 2006: 45)

Hence, in this sense, the different statements that have been identified through the analysis seem to stabilize each other's boundaries so as to entail a mutually reifying relationship. This is, the meaning of one statement is determined by its relationship to other propositions, the constitution of the objects it names and establishes might be defined by further regularities. As Foucault puts it, "the identity of a statement is subjected to a [...] group of conditions [...] that are imposed by all other statements among which it figures" (Foucault [1970] 2010: 103).

To turn to the associated domains of knowledge, the fourth statement inscribed itself more explicitly in the academic domains of history and International Relations compared to the three statements already discussed, while also drawing on knowledge from economic disciplines about the alleged connection between prosperity and market economy. To reproduce the statement in an authoritative way, one would thus have to occupy the position of a historian or IR scholar, or alternatively of a practitioner in the field of development or "democracy promotion", who disposes over "empirical" knowledge about diverging levels of development or advancement. Finally, the repeatable materiality of the statement that allows for it to be inscribed in sense-perceptible elements can be described as a combination of scholarly publications, academic institutions, "democracy promotion" agencies and the programs they set up in "third-world" countries as well as the institutions and procedures involved in the reproduction of EU external relations and development more generally.

3.3 Preliminary Conclusions

Against the backdrop of such a magnitude of regularities and conditions imposing themselves upon our object of interest and the discursive field where it appears, how can we summarize the regularities, exclusions and borders of the (reasonably) speakable in contemporary discourse (cf. above 1.1)? How is "democracy" constituted as a discursive object? Who can speak about it? What knowledge underpins its borders (cf. above 2.1)? Let us start with the questions about stabilizing domains of knowledge. In the JCMS text corpus, democracy emerges as a part of wide field of objects whose existence draws certainty from truth procedures established and knowledge produced in social science disciplines – political sciences, law, economics, social philosophy, ethics, international relations. In terms of the rules according to which truth can be established and discursive object brought forth and delimited, an occupation with isolating the "political fact" and its "reasons" through valid conceptual and statistical representation was identified, as was also a recurring occupation with "normative" procedures defining conditions for the "legitimacy" of governance techniques or arrangements and with procedures for measuring their "efficiency" (cf. 3.11).

What conclusions about the constitution of "democracy" as an object of discourse did the analysis render? To begin with, the analysis of the rules of formation identified different patterns of equations, contrastations and grids of specification recurring throughout the circulation of sentences. Here, democracy was frequently linked to other normatively connoted objects (peace, prosperity, development, justice) and a set of identity descriptions (EU, Europe, the West), while being putting it in opposition to other objects (authoritarianism, autocracy, dictatorship, communism, nationalism, fundamentalism, populism, extremism). High-quality, first-world, advanced democratic societies or states were also repeatedly juxtaposed to various descriptions of less "developed" or less "advanced" entities (cf. 3.12). Furthermore, four statements (enoncés) were identified that help bring forth "democracy" as something intelligible and delineate the borders of the (reasonably) speakable in the context of the text corpus by circumscribing its boundaries in relationship to other objects. First, individual sentences and articulations were tied together though an underlying equation between democracy, political representation, general elections and party pluralism, and a resulting constitution of the term, as referring to or rather consisting of "competitive electoral systems". This equation was related to a perception that democratic procedures fulfill the aim of creating a correspondence between citizen preferences and "policy outcomes", with competition for voter sympathies being seen to ensure the accountability of democratic political leaders, thus making them distinguishable from autocrats, dictators, aristocracy or any other kind of (illegitimate) elite rule.

Thereafter, a second regularity was identified that added constraints and narrowed the realm of the reasonably speakable about democracy by constituting the term as contingent on a range of institutional and legal safeguards against the dangers of power concentration, abuse, polarization and violence: individual and minority rights, the division of (political) power, the subjection of "political leaders" to the rule of law, processes of scrutiny between political institutions and by independent civil society actors (3.22). In other words, democracy is seen to necessitate procedures for creating a peaceful balance between a plurality of societal forces, limiting and dividing political power and channeling conflictuality. A similar concern about preventing established political procedures from "degenerating" so as to threaten the stability and trust in political institutions and elites informed a further, third statement (3.23), which was concerned with the exclusion of political positions that are perceived of as "irrational", "uneducated" or "irresponsible". As a result, any political position too distant from an imagined middle of the political spectrum as defined by contemporary perceptions ("extremism"), and any antagonistic, anti-elite articulation ("populism") were excluded from the reasonably sayable about democratic governance. Notions about the possibility of rational, inclusive deliberation with the potential of improving citizen preferences figured as one solution to these political maladies, while collective identity, communal identification a sense of belonging or demos appeared as sources of commitment to participate in official political processes and of willingness to submit to their outcomes.

Finally, the fourth regularity that we discussed was the recurring interconnected constitutions of democracy as a European or Western value/principle/norm and as something that characterized an advanced stage of societal, historical development (3.24). This regularity, in turn, stabilizes a perception that the EU engages in ethical, normatively desirable behavior when trying to "export" democracy to less advanced societies by "non-coercive" foreign policy techniques.

In terms of the discursive boundaries delimiting such perceptions, a series of ordering structures that produce a discursive divide of the social by assigning things and objects to disjunct comprehensive systems was found to inform both the statements and rules of formation (3.23). The division state/society functioned as a prerequisite for attributing power and the risks of its abused to the state apparatus rather than to any other actors, while society was perceived to be the target of power exertion and a check on state power. The constitution of politics/economy as separate societal spheres which follow different logics and ought to be judged by different criteria instead serves as an underlying prerequisite for "democracy" to be understood as an important principle for describing and normatively judging political processes and institutions, but a meaningless term when applied to economic relations, distribution or domination; that is, as irrelevant to knowledge production about economic realities. The same goes for the distinction public/private, which similarly delineates groups of objects in relationship to which speaking about "democracy" would either make sense or seem like nonsense or mere noise rather than intelligible speech.

To put it bluntly: speaking about "democratic economy", "a democratic working contract", "democratic distribution of wealth", "a democratic family" and so forth does not make sense in the context of the described regularities. Instead, intelligible speech about democracy is concerned with the modalities, reasons and legitimacy of power exertion by the state apparatus in the realm of public, political affairs. Or even more specifically, most often with limiting repressive modes of power exertion and domination by the state (cf. 3.13).

The subject positions necessary for any given subject to occupy in order to reproduce the described discursive regularities and the enunciative modalities that one would have to adhere to oscillated between the social-science scholar and the two more latent positions of the practitioner and the "neutral" moral subject. In all variations, the scholar or academic was defined as speaking subject by her/his distance to discursive objects and her/her proximity to disciplines of knowledge production bringing forth discursive objects, grids of specification (cf. above 3.14) and constituting the associated domains of the respective statements (cf. above 3.21-4). That is, the distance and non-affiliation with the "empirical" objects of which s/he speaks functioned as a condition for him/her to see and speak "truth" about them. In sentences concerned with normative questions, a similar position was identified, from which imagined subjects who do not "know their social position", reside behind a "veil of ignorance" or possess the ability to speak without being biased by interest of coercion, were deemed to be able to reason truthfully about the just, fair organization of society. Interestingly, the position of the practitioner, on the contrary, derived his/her ability to speak truth about discursive objects from his/her involvement with and proximity to their "empirical" existence (cf. above 3.14).

4 Democracy in 19th Century Liberalism: A Walk to the Archive

If the regularities discussed above determine what is reasonably speakable about democracy in the context of contemporary EU governance and the examined social-science text corpus, how did such boundaries emerge historically? Have words kept their meaning, have values and norms kept a fixed content over the course of time? If we were to leave the present for a brief excursion into the historical archive to look at a body of historical text material concerned with the art of government in Europe, legitimacy and democracy, what continuities or breaches could we discern in the perceptions and regularities characterizing the discursive constitution of the term and surrounding, connected regularities? The following sections sketch out some regularities common to John Stuart Mill's "On Liberty" (1859) and "Considerations on Representative Government" (1861), Benjamin Constant's "De la liberté des Anciens comparée à celle des Modernes" (1819) and Alexis de Tocqueville's "Democracy in America" (1835).

As noted earlier, these texts from 19th-century classical liberal political philosophy are concerned with defining legitimate modes of government, with understanding how government and society function and the way such questions relate to the term "democracy". Hence, at least on the first glance this second body of texts resembles the JCMS text material. Rather than repeating a systematic analysis of quite the same magnitude as the one conducted above, in the following I highlight some points of interest: a few regularities, breaches and continuities that present themselves when one compares the two text corpuses and that appeared to me to be of particular relevance in grasping the historical specificity of contemporary perceptions and the disparity and impurity of their "numberless beginnings" (Foucault 1977: 145).

This stroll in the archive, as emphasized above (2.2), should not be confused with, and indeed operates in opposition to, any search for the origins or the historical truth about democracy. Instead, it represents a genealogical excursion into some aspects of the "complex course of descent" (Foucault 1977: 145), a tactical move to illustrate the historical contingency of contemporary regularities of speech. In discussing the rules of formation, I concentrate on the formation of objects, equations, opposition and grids of specification (4.11) and the question of what underlying discursive divisions are at play in assigning objects to comprehensive systems (4.12). I then briefly touch upon the enunciative modalities (4.13) before proceeding to the definition of statements (4.2). Finally, by way of conclusion, I synthesize, compare and discuss the findings from archeological, genealogical, contemporary and historical steps of the investigation (5).

4.1 Rules of formation

4.1.1 *Discursive Objects and Their Relations: False Familiarities*

Although not quite as encompassing, the field of objects in which "democracy" emerges and circulates in our historical text corpus includes a series of elements that one might recognize from contemporary discourse. In particular, objects stemming from knowledge domains concerned with political systems, political philosophy and law circulate prominently and recur across the texts, including "representation", "representatives", "the people", "citizen", "election", "votes", "insti-tutions", "individual rights", "justice", "tyranny", "despotism", "oppre-ssion", "sovereignty", "executive power", "constitution", "public opinion", "freedom of the press" or "peace". However, in many respects, the apparent familiarity of objects and their constellation proves to be deceptive. Objects that seem to belong to knowledge domains which have since been forgotten, discarded or transformed, that have thus lost their sense of having an obvious or natural meaning, or that might seem misplaced in a "scientific" discussion about democracy and government to the contemporary reader also circulate in the texts; for instance, "barbarians", "the savage", "the indian", "the social body", "species", "cultivation", "glory", "inclinations", "prejudice", "passion" and "love". Moreover, even seemingly familiar objects often prove to be Janus-faced – to have unstable borders and to have taken on new meanings over the course of time – once one embarks on considering the patterns of opposition, equation and specification that determine the relationships between them.

In the texts, "representative government" is associated with the "virtues" or "benefits" of "liberty", "freedom", "modernity", "peace", "enlightenment", "commerce" and "individual rights" (Constant 1819: 2-10; Mill 1861: 2-3, 12-13), thus echoing some of the discursive connections that were identified in contemporary speech (cf. in particular 3.12, 3.24). These objects in turn are often associated with notions of advancement and seen as results of historical progress – as constituent parts of "a stage of progress into which the more civilized portions of the species have now entered" (Mill 1859: 10). In this context, a related set of hierarchical identity descriptions comes into play, contrasting the "enlightened", "Christian", "civilized" nations of Europe with "barbarian hordes", "the savage", "the indian" and "the less civilized" (de Tocqueville 1835: 32-3; Constant 1819: 3; Mill 1859: 13-14). However, as a rather stark point of divergence from the present, the term "democracy" does not figure as a part of the described continua of virtues which are attributed to the civilized and enlightened. On the contrary, often "democracy" even appears as a principle or object threatening liberty, representative government, peace and civilization; it is asserted to have "lawless passions", to bring about dangers of "disorder and the agitation of conflict", to carry the risk that "all the laws of moral analogy to be dissolved" (de Tocqueville 1935: 21) or to:

"abandon [the people] to its wild propensities, and [to grow] up like those outcasts who receive their education in the public streets, and who are unacquainted with aught but the vices and wretchedness of society." (de Tocqueville 1835: 17)

In contrast to contemporary orders of speech, "democracy" is therefore neither connected to "competition", "transparency" or "accountability", nor is it seen to necessitate "elections" or entail any close, necessary relationship with "representation". Instead, democracy is repeatedly connected with the terms "equality" and "revolution" (cf. for instance, de Tocqueville 1835: 16, 66, 72; Mill 1861: 81-100, in particular 83). Adding to the confusion of the contemporary reader, the latter terms are not primarily associated with the formal, legal equality of citizens in the political realm that was seen as a vital component of democracy in the analysis of contemporary texts (cf. 3.13). Rather, democracy is repeatedly connected to equality in "eduction", "fortune" and "social conditions", as well as with a resulting increase in the power of the "poorest and the weakest" (de Tocqueville 1935: 16, 70, 15, cf. also 14-18). For instance, de Tocqueville describes "democracy" in terms of a "great revolution" spreading across the Christian world that is "sooner or later" to bring about "an almost complete equality of conditions" (cf. 1835: 14-17, 72-

3). Or, as another sentence reads:

“nothing can satisfy [nations whose *social condition* is democratic] except equality, and rather than lose it they resolve to perish (1835: 72, emphasis added).

Further articulations speak of “democratic representation” and “representative democracy” in ways that might seem to converge more with contemporary regularities of speech (Mill 1961: 82-99). However, once again, the seeming familiarity of such expressions proves to be misleading. Upon closer examination, democracy is not equated with representation as such in the said text passages, but instead “representation” can be more or *less* “democratic”, universal suffrage is interchangeably characterized as “democratic” and “equal” representation and when figuring as a noun, democracy is associated with “the equality of all citizens” (Mill 1861: 80, cf. also 81, 113).

In terms of structuring oppositions, a series of conceptual pairs recurs throughout the text, lending certainty to the boundaries between discursive objects and often helping to hierarchically juxtapose and subordinate democracy to responsible, moderate, representative government. Such dichotomizations include “uneducated”/“knowledgeable”, “wild”/“moderate”, “prejudice”/“enlightenment”, “immoral”/“moral”, “passion”/“rationality”, “disorder”/“harmony”, “agitation of conflict”/“peace” and “liberty”/“authority”. With view to its relationship to other objects, “democracy” is primarily contrasted with “aristocracy” and “monarchy”, but also with “the influence of individuals” over society and arrangements where any “superior class [...] forms the centre of political action” (de Tocqueville 1835: 65-66). Instead of being associated with order, stability or trust in “elites”, as in contemporary speech (cf. 3.11, 3.22-3), demoracy is hence constituted as revolutionary change, an economically and socially vested kind of power of the lower classes and as opposed to elite rule or “aristocracy”:

“Is it credible that the democracy which has annihilated the feudal system and vanquished kings will respect the citizen and the capitalist? Will it stop now that it has grown so strong and its adversaries so weak? None can say which way we are going, for all terms of comparison are wanting: the equality of conditions is more complete in the Christian countries of the present day than it has been at any time or in any part of the world; so that the extent of what already exists prevents us from foreseeing what may be yet to come." (de Tocqueville 1835: 16)

"The social condition of the Americans is eminently democratic; this was its character at the foundation of the Colonies, and is still more strongly marked at the present day. I have stated in the preceding chapter that great equality existed among the emigrants who settled on the shores of New England. The germ of aristocracy was never planted in that part of the Union." (de Tocqueville 1835: 65).

Finally, the relationship between "democracy" and "liberty" constitutes a point of uncertainty and concern in the texts. In contrast to "democracy", the term "liberty" is attributed with a strong positive normative connotation. It figures in close conjunction with "justice" and "legitimacy", while being constituted as an opposite of "tyranny", "despotism" and "[state] authority" and is closely connected to the individual subject and objects that are seen to refer to an absence of state interference in the activities of citizens: "I'll say it again: the true modern liberty is individual liberty" (Constant 1819: 10, cf. also 6-9, 12; Tocqueville 1835: 50-199; Mill 1859: 9, 12-3). Moreover, liberty is often perceived to be protected through "representation", "responsible government", limitations and scrutiny of political power, the establishment and protection of individual and minority rights (Constant 1819: 10, 12; Mill 1859: 9, 12-3). What relationship is this kind of freedom perceived to entail to the burgeoning revolutionary spread of social equality that the texts implicitly understand by the term "democracy"? While some sentences in the texts seek for ways of combining the terms, the objects seem far from entailing any harmonic relationship:

"Not that those nations whose social condition is democratic naturally despise liberty; on the contrary, they have an instinctive love of it. But liberty is not the chief and constant object of their desires; equality is their idol." (de Tocqueville 1835: 72)

Other text passages instead reflect a more explicit concern with "saving" liberty from the risks posed by "democracy", which are understood to include chaos and conflict, "political despotism", "tyranny" over the individual and class legislation (cf. Mill 1859: 13-4; 1861: 81). A terminology similar to that of representation, individual and minority rights, constraints and checks on political power that was intimately connected with democracy in our contemporary text corpus (cf. above 3.12, 3.22), in this historical textuality is thus instead perceived of as safeguards against the evils and risks "democracy" itself might bring about.

4.1.2 *Comprehensive Systems*

What underlying distinctions could be said to delineate such perceptions? How are discursive objects ordered by assignment to comprehensive systems? The connections and contrasts just discussed point to a different regularity of assigning "democracy" to broader categories than in contemporary speech. Notably, intelligible speech drawing on, naming and constituting democracy as a descriptive category or principle is not limited to the political realm or state institutions. Rather, democracy is imagined as equality and a kind of power – of the people, the poor or the majority – that take on economic and societal forms. Its existence is not contingent on a particular kind of state or political institution: "The existence of a democracy was seemingly unknown, when on a sudden it took possession of the supreme power [French Revolution]" (de Tocqueville 1835: 17). Hence, "a democracy" is perceived of as being compatible with, or rather able to establish, different forms of organizing sociopolitical reality rather than as signifying a certain kind of polity or political system. As Tocqueville explains:

"I am far from supposing that [the Americans] have chosen the only form of government which a democracy may adopt." (1835: 16)

Formulated in more general terms, the opposition between "politics" and "the economy" which was identified as an implicit, stabilizing division structuring contemporary speech is not as present in the historical text corpus. For instance, economic distribution is perceived to have immediate consequences for the proper categorization of a given polity, and political measures affecting distribution of resources are described in the same vocabulary as political institutions:

"[...] this law unites, draws together, and vests property and power in a few hands: its tendency is clearly aristocratic" (de Tocqueville 1835: 66, cf. also 46, 65, 629).

That is, the difference between "aristocracy" and "democracy" is not merely understood in terms of, say, an opposition between general, free and fair elections and limited suffrage, but is defined more broadly as "conferring great privileges on a small number of persons" or "privileges [being] acquired by all" (Tocqueville 1835: 623). Hence, the distinction between democracy and aristocracy becomes not solely a question of political power or mandates, the modalities of its allocation and exertion: rather, assigning a polity or a society to either category (democratic, aristocratic) demands a consideration of the *overall* distribution of political and economic power, resources and other privileges in a society.

What, then, of the distinctions between society/state, and public/private that were also deemed powerful in delineating the reasonably sayable in the context of contemporary regularities? Let us start with the former. While the historical texts investigated tend to assign "democracy" to society rather than the state in a way that diverges significantly from contemporary regularities, a continuity might be identified in how the state is imagined as the principle center of authority, the locus of power and thus also as the primary source of tyranny and power abuse (cf. above 3.13). This implicit imaginary functions as a prerequisite for "liberty" to be understood in terms of individual freedom from the state in the way that the following quote might illustrate:

"The aim, therefore, of patriots, was to set limits to the power which the ruler should be suffered to exercise over the community; and this limitation was what they meant by liberty." (Mill 1859: 10)

Therefore, the state/society distinction and the notion of power as oppression emanating from political authority, rather than any productive, ideational or economic force, seems to constitute a continuity between the text corpuses (cf. above 3.13, 3.24). The same goes for the distinction public/private: the texts are underpinned by a concern with upholding such a separation. To illustrate, the primary source of legitimacy for representative government is imagined to be its function as a check against the invasion of public affairs into the sphere of privacy:

"So power must accept the facts: we need liberty and we shall have it. But since the liberty we need is different from that of the ancients, it needs to be organized differently from ancient liberty. In the latter, the more time and energy a man dedicated to exercising his political rights, the freer he thought himself to be; whereas with the kind of liberty we can have, the more the exercise of political rights leaves us the time for our private interests, the more precious liberty will be to us. Hence the need for the representative system. It is nothing but an organization by means of which a nation charges a few individuals to do what it can't or doesn't want to do itself." (Constant 1819: 2-3)

Finally, a further structuring division that implicitly supports an argument of the above kind seems to be a strict separation between the collective and the individual, with the collective figuring as an aggregation of pre-given individualities and a potential means of (illegitimate) domination of one or more over others, rather than, for instance, as the origin of persons themselves. Hence, freedom or liberty can be categorized as a state achievable by, or a quality belonging to, the individual, while the only legitimate function of the collective becomes restraining the domination of which it is itself the (potential) source:

"The only freedom which deserves the name, is that of pursuing our own good in our own way, so long as we do not attempt to deprive others of theirs, or impede their efforts to obtain it." (Mill 1859: 12)

4.1.3 *The Enunciative Modalities*

How do the enunciative modalities, the issue of who is qualified to speak such sentences, implied in the historical text corpus compare to the contemporary positions of the social scientist, the neutral moral subject and the practitioner? On the one hand, any subject (re)producing the speech discussed above must be in possession of a similar kind of knowledge as the social-scientist position discussed in the context of contemporary regularities; s/he must have access to truth about society, history, the law and the state. One the other hand, the techniques for establishing and producing truths about the said objects differ from the present: there is no similar exercise in varying factors, no equivalent concern with proving causality or with producing unbiased statistical representation. Rather, truth is established by a combination of reasoning, personal observation and references to works or œuvres produced by wise, educated men.

The separation between the practitioner and the social scientist hence seems to dissolve in a position that might be best described as a *Gelehrter*—that is, the educated "savant" (Mill 1861: 35), the wise man of letters, the "intelligent thinker" (Mill 1859: 8). To illustrate the difference to the (social) scientist, rather than measuring equality by indexes and data collection, de Tocqueville draws on his personal travels to "the

Americas", on his personal observational skills, physical presence and engagement with the object of interest to lend certainty to the claim: "I observed that the equality of conditions is daily progressing" (1835: 13). Hence, non-interference with the measured reality, the isolation of factors and uncovering of effects through variation do not constitute criteria for attributing authority to a proposition. Rather, truth is established through analysis of the consequences of maxims, the assump-tions supporting arguments, by tempered observation and ordering differentiation:

"Montesquieu, whose mind was more observant because he wasn't such a hot-head, didn't fall right into the same errors. He was struck by the differences I have described, but he didn't discover their true cause. According to him, the Greek politicians who lived under the popular government didn't recognize any power but the power of (1) virtue. Politicians today tell us only about (2) manufactures, commerce, finances, wealth and even luxury. He attributes this difference to the difference between (1) the republic and (2) the monarchy. It ought instead to be attributed to the difference, indeed the oppositeness, between (1) the spirit of ancient times and (2) the spirit of modern times." (Constant 1819: 7-8)

Hence, the relationship of the savant or *Gelehrter* to society as a whole can be described as combination of education and intellect, with truth procedures in a sense being more closely tied to a holistic view of the speaking person, to "superior intellect and character" (Mill 1961: 80) than in contemporary speech. Moreover, the authority of the speaking subject often appears to be more explicitly connected to his social position in the sense of belonging to "the most powerful, the most intelligent, and the most moral classes of the nation" (de Tocqueville 1835: 18). Lastly, and not very surprisingly, the speaking subject is ethnically and culturally European, with truth and science being constituted as an occupation reserved for "men of intellect" who belong to the "civilized portions" of the human species (Mill 1961: 11).

4.2 Statements

As with the previous analysis of contemporary text material, let us proceed to defining some of the underlying structuring assumptions that delineate what is reasonably "speakable" within the text corpus. That is, we want to ask what assumptions about "democracy" and related discursive objects recur across texts and sentences, what borders serve as implicit conditions of diverging articulations and how these can be summarized in the form of statements (enoncés). At the risk of repeating myself, it is nonetheless important to stress the point that the "historical conditions required if one is to 'say anything'" (Foucault [1970] 2010: 44) in any given discursive constellation are by far too many and too obscure to be exhaustively treated in a context such as the present investigation. Instead of making any claims about completeness, I have thus chosen to discuss two interconnected regularities in some more detail which uncover points of rapture, continuity and transformation compared to contemporary regularities of speech, so as to illustrate the disparity of beginnings, the historical contingency of discursive constitution and the ambivalence and accidental nature of its transformation. As the respective "subject positions" necessary to re-produce the statements do not differ in any significant way from the enunciative modalities discussed above, the discussion concentrates on the conceptual dimensions of the "referential", the "associated domain" and the "repeatable materiality" (Foucault [1970] 2010: 88-105), while comparing these points to the statements and borders that were identified in the JCMS body of text.

4.2.1 *Democratic Revolution and Equality: Dangers of Anarchy and Despotism*

> "The democracy of France, checked in its course or abandoned to its lawless passions, has overthrown whatever crossed its path, and has shaken all that it has not destroyed. Its empire on society has not been gradually introduced or peaceably established, but it has constantly advanced in the midst of disorder and the agitation of a conflict. [...] I cannot recall to my mind a passage in history more worthy of sorrow and of pity than the scenes which are happening under our eyes; it is as if the natural bond which unites the opinions of man to his tastes and his actions to his principles was now broken; the sympathy which has always been acknowledged between the feelings and the ideas of mankind appears to be dissolved, and all the laws of moral analogy to be dissolved, and all the laws of moral analogy to be abolished." (de Tocqueville 1835: 21)

> "The men whom the flow of events swept to the head of our revo-

lution were—inevitably, given the education they had received—steeped in ancient views that have become false, views that Rousseau and de Mably had made respectable. Rousseau's metaphysics, in the middle of which there are sudden flashes of sublime truth, and passages of stirring eloquence; and Mably's austerity: his intolerance, his hatred of all human passions, his eagerness to enslave everyone, his extravagant principles about what the law can achieve, the difference between what he recommended and what had previously existed, his denunciation of wealth and even of property; —all these things were bound to charm men who were lit up by a recent victory, and who, having gained control of the law's power, were happy about the idea of extending this power to everything." (Constant 1819: 8)

"It has been seen that the dangers incident to a representative democracy are of two kinds: danger of a low grade of intelligence in the representative body, and in the popular opinion which controls it; and danger of class legislation on the part of the numerical majority, these being all composed of the same class." (Mill 1861: 81)

"Still, the great proprietors south of the Hudson constituted a superior class, having ideas and tastes of its own, and forming the centre of political action. This kind of aristocracy sympathized with the body of the people." (de Tocqueville 1835: 65)

"[...] democratic tendencies were awakened; and having thrown off the yoke of the mother country, it aspired to independence of every kind. The influence of individuals gradually ceased to be felt, and custom and law united together to produce the same result." (de Tocqueville 1835: 66)

"Is it credible that the democracy which has annihilated the feudal system and vanquished kings will respect the citizen and the capitalist? Will it stop now that it has grown so strong and its adversaries so weak? None can say which way we are going, for all terms of comparison are wanting: the equality of conditions is more complete in the Christian countries of the present day than it has been at any time or in any part of the world; so that the extent of what already exists prevents us from foreseeing what may

> be yet to come.” (de Tocqueville 1835: 16)
>
> “There is a country in the world where the great revolution which I am speaking of seems nearly to have reached its natural limits [...] It appears to me beyond a doubt that sooner or later we shall arrive, like the Americans, at an almost complete equality of conditions.” (de Tocqueville 1835: 17)

A number of commonalities structuring the discursive constitution of democracy as an object in de Tocqueville, Constant and Mill were touched upon in the above discussion of the formation of objects. By considering the various connection and contrasts repeating themselves across the texts, a number of breaches and discontinuities with contemporary perceptions were uncovered (cf. above 4.11). Notably, in the text corpus, democracy is put in close proximity to the term “equality”, rather than to representation, elections or competition (de Tocqueville 1835: 14, 16-7, 70; Mill 1861: 81-100). As Mill parenthetically states, there is a recurring perception that: “[...] the principle of democracy [...] professes equality as its very root and foundation” (Mill 1861: 83). Moreover, democracy is repeatedly seen to belong to the social and economic realm of society, to constitute a kind of power or social force attributed to the poor and unprivileged, rather than being perceived of as signifying any specific kind of polity or arrangement of political institutions (cf. de Tocqueville 1835: 72; Mill 1861: 81-100). In consequence, “democracy” is contrasted with and seen as opposed to “elite rule” and “aristocracy” in political, social and economical terms. As a further, related discontinuity with contemporary regularities, “democracy” is neither connected with stability nor with trust in established political institutions, mandate holders or procedures. On the contrary, it is perceived as a revolutionary, potentially destructive, intolerant and dangerous force with “wild propensities” that threatens to destabilize the social and moral order which historical progress and civilization is understood to have brought about in the “enlightened”, “civilized” nations (cf. de Tocqueville 1835: 21; Mill 1859: 6; Constant 1819: 7-9).

On the one hand, democracy is therefore associated with anarchy and chaos, “fierce hatreds, conflicting interests, and contending factions”, the destruction of “natural bonds” and dissolution “laws of moral analogy”, all of which are deemed to follow in the wake of revolution (de Tocqueville 1835: 754, 21). On the other hand, sentences and articulations repeatedly assume that democratic revolution towards a "complete equality in conditions" (de Tocqueville 1835: 17) has a inherent tendency towards increasing "the functions of central government" once it has brought it under its control, and to "extend" the "power [of the law] to everything", thus threatening to evolve into a form of political tyranny manifesting itself in "the subjection of individual existence to the collective body", "tyranny of the majority", "collective despotism" and "class legislation" (Constant 1819: 8, 3; Mill 1859: 13; 1861: 94). Thus unchecked democracy appears as a potential source of both anarchy and chaos, political despotism and tyranny.

Adding to these perceptions, a sense of inevitability is also repeatedly attributed to the ascent and spread of democracy across the Christian, civilized world. De Tocqueville, for instance, comments on the future evolution of democracy by stating: "It appears to me beyond a doubt that sooner or later we shall arrive, like the Americans, at an almost complete equality of conditions" (de Tocqueville 1835: 17). Another text passage instead explicitly concludes:

"The Christian nations of our age [...] present a most alarming spectacle; the [democratic] impulse which is bearing them along is so strong that it cannot be stopped" (de Tocqueville 1835: 16).

Finally, democracy, equality and revolution are often connected with terms such as "passion", "inclination", "prejudice" and "ignorance", while the social, moral and/or political order that they are threatening to "destroy" and "dissolve" is described as relying on "intellect", "education" or "morality" (de Tocqueville 1835: 17, 22, 24, 753; Mill 1861: 90-2). That is, democracy is understood to be driven by instincts rather than intellect, passion rather than reason: it is constituted as deriving from an inferior kind of agency or logic in a way that strangely resembles the exclusion of populism, extremism and other "irrational", "uneducated" or "irresponsible" positions in the contemporary text corpus, while representing a reversion of the contemporary connection between democracy, responsibility and rationality (cf. above 3.23). On this basis, a first statement can be formulated which summarizes the regularities forming around the notion of democracy as equality, its revolutionary, lawless and passionate spread and the dangers the latter implies.

Statement A

Across the civilized world, equality in social conditions, education and property is spreading in a revolutionary, passionate and unhalted manner. Having overthrown feudal systems and monarchs, this democratic revolution operates in opposition to elite power in political, social and economic manifestations; it threatens to dissolve moral and social order and carries the dangers of conflict and anarchy, political despotism, class legislation and the subjugation of the individual to the collective.

What epistemic conditions can be deemed to constitute the "referential" of such a regularity, its "laws of possibility, rules of existence for the objects and relations" (Foucault [1970] 2010: 91) which it names, establishes or denies? To start with, the regularities expressed by the above formulation presume an equation between democracy and equality, as well as an understanding of the latter as pertaining to socio-economic aspects of societal reality besides potential political consequences of its spread. Moreover, oppositions between "reason" and "impulse", "sense" and "sensibility", "education" and "ignorance", "rudeness" and "cultivation" stabilize and bring forth contrasting hierarchical perceptions of democracy as uncontrolled, wild, instinct-driven, uneducated and rude (de Tocqueville 1835: 753) – whilst the moral and social order it is threatening to destroy and the elite rule by the "most intelligent and most moral classes" (de Tocqueville: 1835: 17) which it is perceived to negate are understood to be based on superior ratio, education and morality – or in alternative wording on "superior intellects and characters" (Mill 1861: 91). That is, the perception of democracy as a revolution in societal equality is not necessary connected with any implicit normative or political affirmation of such a development, but on the contrary with an underlying anxiety about what further societal evolution and destruction it might bring about, what "order", "sophistication", "intelligence" and "liberty" might be destroyed by its advancement:

"Is it credible that the democracy which has annihilated the feudal system and vanquished kings will respect the citizen and the capitalist?" (de Tocqueville 1835: 16; cf. also Mill 1859: 13-5; 1861: 81-6).

A further, structuring condition for a statement such as the above to emerge and be reproduced seems to me to be the distinction between the individual and the collective that was touched upon above (4.12). With freedom and liberty being understood as a quality belonging to the individual, and the only legitimate function of the collective being identified as restraining domination over the individual, power of the majority over the rich or an abolition of elite rule might be perceived in terms of "tyranny", "subjugation" or "despotism".

With a view to the associated domains, certainty about the statements representative content relies on is stabilized by knowledge about the historical development and progression of society, about the course of civilization, but also about different polities and states, about law and morality. Moreover, these domains encompass propositions about human passions, hatred, instincts, charm, intellectual refinement and so forth, thus encompassing a kind of knowledge that would probably be categorized as "psychology" in contemporary speech but that does not appear as a separate knowledge domain in the text corpus. What repeatable materiality allows for the statement to be reproduced in physical or sense-perceptible sense? On the one hand, as with all statements discussed so far, the repeatable materiality consists of the academic institutions, universities and text productions where knowledge drawn upon is produced. In this case: the systems of higher education, universities, modes of interaction between scholars and publications in 19th-century Britain and France. On the other hand, the statement also inscribes itself in the material or sense-perceptible reality through the existence of the very institutions and social processes it is "making sense of": the relative disempowerment of feudal systems and monarchs, and the revolutionary struggles of the 18th and 19th century.

4.2.2 *The Need for a Representative System and Limitations on Power: Protecting Liberty and Educating Democracy*

> "The struggle between Liberty and Authority is the most conspicuous feature in the portions of history with which we are earliest familiar, particularly in that of Greece, Rome, and England. But in old times this contest was between subjects, or some classes of subjects, and the government. By liberty, was meant protection against the tyranny of the political rulers." (Mill 1859: 9)
>
> "I'll say it again: the true modern liberty is individual liberty. Po-

litical liberty is its guarantee, which is why we must have political liberty too. But to ask today's peoples to sacrifice their entire individual liberty to political liberty, as the ancients did, is the surest means of detaching them from the latter, after which it won't take long to rob them of the former." (Constant 1819: 10-1)

"The only freedom which deserves the name, is that of pursuing our own good in our own way, so long as we do not attempt to deprive others of theirs, or impede their efforts to obtain it." (Mill 1859: 22)

"The only purpose for which power can be rightfully exercised over any member of a civilized community, against his will, is to prevent harm to others. [...] The only part of the conduct of any one, for which he is amenable to society, is that which concerns others. In the part which merely concerns himself, his independence is, of right, absolute. Over himself, over his own body and mind, the individual is sovereign. It is, perhaps, hardly necessary to say that this doctrineis meant to apply only to human beings in the maturity of their faculties. We are not speaking of children, or of young persons below the age which the law may fix as that of manhood or womanhood. Those who are still in a state to require being taken care of by others, must be protected against their own actions as well as against external injury. For the same reason, we may leave out of consideration those backward states of society in which the race itself may be considered as in its nonage. The early difficulties in the way of spontaneous progress are so great, that there is seldom any choice of means for overcoming them; and a ruler full of the spirit of improvement is warranted in the use of any expedients that will attain an end, perhaps otherwise unattainable." (Mill 1859: 18-19)

"Despotism is a legitimate mode of government in dealing with barbarians, provided the end be their improvement, and the means justified by actually effecting that end. Liberty, as a principle, has no application to any state of things anterior to the time when mankind have become capable of being improved by free and equal discussion. Until then, there is nothing for them but implicit obedience to an Akbar or a Charlemagne, if they are so fortunate as to find one." (Mill 1859: 19)

"Even the division of Europe into distinct states is more apparent than real, thanks to the spread of enlightenment. Back then, each people constituted an isolated family, the born enemy of other families; whereas now there is a mass of human beings that have the same basic nature, though with different names and forms of social organization. This mass is strong enough to have nothing to fear from barbarian hordes. It is enlightened enough to find war a burden. Its uniform tendency is towards peace." (Constant 1819: 3)

"So power must accept the facts: we need liberty and we shall have it. [...] Hence the need for the representative system. It is nothing but an organization by means of which a nation charges a few individuals to do what it can't or doesn't want to do itself. Poor men look after their own affairs; rich ones hire stewards. [...] But, unless they are idiots, rich men who employ stewards keep a close and strict watch on whether they are doing their duty, [...] In the same way, the people who resort to the representative system so as to enjoy the liberty that suits them, should exercise an active and constant surveillance over their representatives, and reserve for themselves the right – at times that aren't too far apart – to discard them if they betray their trust, and to revoke any powers they have abused." (Constant 1819: 12)

"The aim, therefore, of patriots, was to set limits to the power which the ruler should be suffered to exercise over the community; and this limitation was what they meant by liberty. It was attempted in two ways. First, by obtaining a recognition of certain immunities, called political liberties or rights. [...] A second, and generally a later expedient, was the establishment of constitutional checks; by which the consent of the community, or of a body of some sort supposed to represent its interests, was made a necessary condition to some of the more important acts of the governing power." (Mill 1859: 10)

"A time, however, came, in the progress of human affairs, when men ceased to think it a necessity of nature that their governors should be an independent power, opposed in interest to themselves. It appeared to them much better that the various magistrates of the State should be their tenants or delegates, revocable at their pleasure. In that way alone, it seemed, could they have complete security that the powers of government would never be abused to their disadvantage. By degrees this new demand for elective and temporary rulers became the prominent object of the exertions of the popular party, wherever any such party existed; and superseded, to a considerable extent, the previous efforts to limit the power of rulers. As the struggle proceeded for making the ruling power emanate from the periodical choice of the ruled, some persons began to think that too much importance had been attached to the limitation of the power itself." (Mill 1859: 6)

> "Every individual being in the possession of rights which he is sure to retain, a kind of manly reliance and reciprocal courtesy would arise between all classes, alike removed from pride and meanness. The people, well acquainted with its true interests, would allow that in order to profit by the advantages of society it is necessary to satisfy its demands. In this state of things the voluntary association of the citizens might supply the individual exertions of the nobles, and the community would be alike protected from anarchy and from oppression. I admit that, in a democratic State thus constituted, society will not be stationary; but the impulses of the social body may be regulated and directed forwards." (de Tocqueville 1835: 19)

> "The first duty which is at this time imposed upon those who direct our affairs is to educate the democracy; to warm its faith, if that be possible; to purify its morals; to direct its energies; to substitute a knowledge of business for its inexperience, and an acquaintance with its true interests for its blind propensities; to adapt its government to time and place, and to modify it in compliance with the occurrences and the actors of the age. A new science of politics is indispensable to a new world." (de Tocqueville 1835: 16-7)

A further regularity that is worth considering in this context concerns the constitution of the relationship between "democracy" and "liberty" in the text corpus. As was touched upon earlier and as some of the quotes above serve to illustrate, the texts repeatedly contrast “liberty” with terms such as “[state] authority”, “political tyranny” and “collective despotism”, while placing it in close conjuncture with the individual subject and an absence of state interference in the private affairs of citizens (cf. above 4.11; Mill 1859: 6, 9; Constant 1819: 10-11; de Tocqueville 1835: 21). Moreover, liberty is connected with the superior “stage of civilization” which historical progress is understood to have brought about in the enlightened nations of Europe where “the more civilized portions of the [human] species” reside (Mill 1859: 10, 13-14; de Tocqueville 1835: 32-3; Constant 1819: 3). On the one hand, liberty is seen as a product of such historical advancement (cf. Mill 1859: 11; de Tocqueville 1835). On the other hand, its applicability as a principle of justice is also understood to be limited to enlightened, advanced subjects; “to apply only to human beings in the maturity of their faculties”, thus excluding children and young people, individuals not able to care for themselves and notably:

“those backward-states of society in which the race itself may be considered as in its nonage. [...] Despotism is a legitimate mode of government in dealing with barbarians, provided the end be their improvement.” (Mill 1859: 19)

Objects such as representative government, limitations on political power, constitutional checks and individual and minority rights repeatedly enter this scene as procedures aiming to protect individual liberty. As Constant states, “So power must accept the facts: we need liberty and we shall have it. [...] Hence the need for a representative system” (1819: 12). Or as Mill explains:

“The aim, therefore, of patriots, was to set limits to the power which the ruler should be suffered to exercise over the community; and this limitation was what they meant by liberty.” (1859: 10)

In contrast to contemporary speech, “democracy” is not included in such continuum, but on the contrary appears as a source of risks, as a wild force endangering such procedures through the spectrum of dangers that the first statement describes as oscillating between anarchy, conflict, revolution, political tyranny and class legislation (Mill 1861: 81; cf. above 3.12, 3.22). It might appear then that democracy ought to be destroyed for liberty to blossom. However, this conclusion is complicated by the recurring perception that the ascent of democracy is somehow inevitable or impossible to halt – an “impulse which is [...] so strong that it cannot be stopped” (de Tocqueville 1835: 16). Rather than imagining any obliteration of democracy as a safeguard for liberty, a number of sentences distributed across the texts instead circulate around the possibility, or indeed rather the necessity, to “educate” and improve democracy so as to *become* more compatible with the virtuous circle of individual liberty, representative government, rights, scrutiny, constitu-tional checks, peace, progress, commerce and modernity that is seen to characterize the “enlightened” and “civilized” societies (cf. Constant 1819: 2-10; Mill 1861: 2-3, 12-13; 1861: 2-3). That is, while democracy is perceived as dangerous, potentially anarchic and despotic, its spread is believed to be incredibly difficult to halt, it is overarchingly believed to be “unexperienced”, “ignorant” and, crucially, its future is perceived as unsure and yet to be decided (de Tocqueville: 1835: 16, 17, 753; Mill 1859). As Tocqueville puts it:

“The Christian nations of our age seem to me to present a most alarming spectacle; the impulse which is bearing them along is so strong that it cannot be stopped, but it is not yet so rapid that it cannot be guided: their fate is in their hands; yet a little while and it may be so no longer.” (Tocqueville 1835)

Hence, there is a recurring sense of necessity and urgency to improve and “educate” democracy rather than to destroy it, to distinguish between “true and false democracy” and to separate the former from any tendency towards political tyranny and class legislation in order to protect liberty and progress (de Tocqueville 1835: 16; Mill 1861: 81-97). To this end, legislators ought to make democracy “fit to govern”, “instruct it and correct its vices” and “the most powerful, the most intelligent, and the most moral classes of the nation [must attempt] to connect themselves with it in order to guide it” (de Tocqueville 1835: 17). In other words, “the first duty which is at this time imposed upon those who direct our affairs” is perceived to be:

“to warm [democracy's] faith, if that be possible; to purify its morals; to direct its energies; to substitute a knowledge of business for its inexperience, and an acquaintance with its true interests for its blind propensities; to adapt its government to time and place, and to modify it in compliance with the occurrences and the actors of the age.” (de Tocqueville 1835: 16-17)

A second regularity of speech in our historical body of text can be formulated which is concerned with liberty and its protection through representative government, individual rights and limitation of power, the dangers that unchecked, uneducated and uncontrolled democracy might pose to such attainments and the resulting necessity to channel its energies, to shape and educate it accordingly.

Statement B

Representative government and limitations on political power, including individual and minority rights, processes of scrutiny and constitutional checks, ultimately serve the legitimate purpose of protecting individual liberty in the enlightened, civilized, European nations. If the spread of democracy across the civilized world is not to undo these attainments, democracy itself must be educated and formed so as to be made fit to govern, to respect the said institutions and to preclude it from degenerating into conflict, anarchy or political tyranny over the individual and the higher, moral and educated classes.

To turn to the referential, a central condition for the statement and sentences reproducing it to emerge as an intelligible part of discourse is the distinction between the civilized, enlightened, cultivated, Christian, European nations, on the one hand, and the "savage" or the "barbarian" on the other. Hence, a hierarchy placing Europe at the forefront of historical progress and an according perception of history as linear and progressive can be identified as an underlying assumption.

To a certain extent, this regularity therefore echoes the hierarchical assumptions that were deemed to underpin identity descriptions and perceptions about international spread of democracy in our contemporary text corpus (cf. above 3.12, 3.24). However, this kind of hierarchization is put in more explicit terms in the historical text corpus, with the imagined distance between the European "stage of civilization" and the "savage" being understood as impossible or extremely hard to bridge. In consequence, improvement of subordinate, uncivilized others is not imagined as a process of immediate assimilation – as in contemporary speech – but rather as a disciplinary exercise: "despotism" is a legitimate and necessary means of improving the "barbarian" and in that context "liberty" does not constitute a relevant, applicable principle.

Furthermore, an understanding of power as oppression emanating from the state or political authority once more seems to underpin the objects and relations that the statement names and brings forth, while liberty as a property of the enlightened and civilized individual subject functions as the only legitimate basis of collective, political arrangements. Finally, the understanding that education has an inherent tendency to let subjects converge towards a universal kind of rationality also seems to underpins the hope that democracy, once educated and enlightened, will realize its "own interests" and hence abandon any violent, radical tendencies towards tyranny or class justice:

"As mankind improve, the number of doctrines which are no longer disputed or doubted will be constantly on the increase: and the well-being of mankind may almost be measured by the number and gravity of the truths which have reached the point of being uncontested." (Mill 1859: 50)

Similar to the first historical statement, the associated domain providing the necessary discursive conditions for the statement to inscribe itself as a meaningful proposition encompasses knowledge about history, the progress of civilization and the workings of the state, the law and human propensities and passions. However, speaking of knowledge, it is also worth noting a sense of necessity to expand scholarly knowledge about democracy in order to "direct its energies" and shape it in the envisioned fashion. As de Tocqueville exclaims, it seems: "A new science of politics is indispensable to a new world." (1835: 17). Finally, as with the first statement, the repeatable materiality in which the statement inscribes itself can be described as a combination of 19th-century British and French systems of higher education, universities, modes of interaction between academic literate authors, formats and procedures of publication and distribution. In addition, the statement inscribes itself in "sense-perceptible" reality through the material existence of the institutions it is naming and reproducing: individual and minority rights, processes of scrutiny and constitutional checks but also colonial, repressive, "despotic" government techniques which European states of the period directed towards unenlightened, non-European "barbarians".

5 Concluding Discussion

"On this basis, it is obvious that Paul Ree was wrong to follow the English tendency in describing the history of morality in terms of linear developments – in reducing its entire history and genesis to an exclusive concern with utility. He assumed that words had kept their meaning, that desire still pointed in a single direction, and that ideas retained their logic; and he ignored the fact that the world of speech and desire has known invasions, struggles, plundering, disguises, ploys." (Foucault 1977: 139)

5.1 The Instability of "Democracy" as a Discursive Object

What overall conclusion can be drawn from the multitude of observations about regularities of contemporary speech in the JCMS text corpus and its continuities and breaches with our historical text material, which the above investigation has allowed us to make? How can we summarize the regularities, exclusions and borders of the (reasonably) speakable about democracy?

Perhaps it is best to start where we began: with the contemporary perception of "democracy" as belonging to a stable set of European norms and values which the EU is seeking to export to other parts of the world, in order to make it "a better place for all" (Van Rompuy/Barroso 2012). The analysis of contemporary regularities of speech and the subsequent genealogical walk to the archives of European political thought proved to put into question and subvert such certainties; on the one hand, by uncovering the specificity of contemporary speech, thus illustrating how discourse inevitably reflects a rarity (Foucault 1972: 119), and on the other hand, by bringing to light the historical contingency and fragility of "democracy" as a "norm", "value", or, better, as an object of discourse. Let us recall some of the said regularities and discontinuities over time in order to illustrate this point.

In the contemporary text corpus, democracy was overarchingly perceived as signifying a normatively superior kind of political system, characterized by a combination of political representation, general elections and party pluralism, which serves the purpose of producing a "match" between "citizen preferences" and "policy outcomes" (cf. 3.21). While accountability, transparency and openness were seen to optimize such arrangement, a further category of objects pertaining to the division and limitation of political power was seen as containing the necessary traits of democratic governance, as creating a balance between societal forces and precluding the eruption of harmful conflictuality, thus adding to the specificity of what democracy is understood to entail and narrowing the borders of the reasonably speakable (cf. 3.22). A further set of limits instead circumscribed the spectrum of political positions or preferences to be included in the democratic political processes in a way that resulted in the exclusion of positions that were perceived as less "rational", "educated" or "responsible" and hence as threatening the stability and trust in political institutions and elites. In particular, populism and extremism figured prominently in this context and were seen to carry the risk of violence, radicalization and "irresponsible" anti-elite discourse (cf. 3.23). These regularities were deemed to stabilize the boundaries of a further statement that places the EU at an advanced stage of societal development, hence bringing forth an understanding that the EU engages in ethical, normatively desirable behavior when trying to export "democracy" to less developed societies by "soft", "civilian" foreign-policy techniques (cf. 3.24).

If the archeological analysis thus revealed some of the specificity and discursive conditions for such perceptions to emerge as regularities of speech, their instability and historical contingency become evident against the backdrop of the genealogical engagement with our historical text corpus. The analyzed texts from 19th-century liberalism and the contemporary social-science text corpus from the JCMS resemble each other in the sense that both discursive constellations revolve around questions about legitimacy of government, the workings of society, history and the law. However, "democracy" turned out to have rather different, in some respects even opposite meanings in the two contexts, to be constituted in different ways in its relationship to other objects through contrasts and equations and to be attributed differently to comprehensive systems. While democracy figured in close proximity to stability and trust in elites in contemporary articulations (3.22, 3.23), textual regularities in our historical corpus associated the term with revolution, social and economic (rather than political) equality and a potentially destructive, anarchic or despotic power of the lower classes (4.11, 4.21). Moreover, many of the objects that were associated with democracy and seen to serve the purpose of channelling conflictuality in contemporary speech – such as representation, individual and minority rights, separation of powers, limitation and scrutiny of political power (cf. 3.22) – in the investigated historical textuality appeared as arrangements aiming to protect individual liberty from the very dangers that the spread of democracy might confront it with if it is not properly educated and transformed (4.22).

However, the genealogical walk to the archive also uncovered points of continuity between historical and contemporary speech. Notably, an underlying understanding of representative government, limitations of political power and so forth, as European attainments reflecting an advanced stage of societal historical development informed both our historical text corpus (4.22) and the identified regularities of contemporary speech (3.24). Although the distance between the European and subordinate others was imagined as greater in historical speech – and improvement understood to entail "despotism" (4.22) rather than incentive structure and soft instrument interventions aiming at immediate assimilation to EU/European values and standards (3.24) – a continuity could still be identified in the implied notions of hierarchy and advancement separating the enlightened and civilized European nations from the "savage" or "barbarian hordes", or to use contemporary vocabulary, distinguishing advanced and developed European political systems from "target countries", "post-communist" or "authoritarian regimes". Other points of continuity included the discursive division of the social realm in state and society, public and private, but also an implicit repressive understanding of power, its attribution to the state apparatus and a resulting concern with limiting power exertion by the state over society in the public realm (cf. 3.13, 4.12).

5.2 Implications and Paths for Future Research

Rather than recalling any further the more specific findings that the investigation rendered, as a final point I would like to touch upon what implications its overall results might be deemed to have for thinking about "democracy", language and power, and also for further research at the nexus of discourse analysis, European integration and IR. The historical contingency of the discursive constitution of "democracy", which the genealogical step of our analysis illustrated, and the ensuing subversion of contemporary perceptions that "democracy" constitutes a stable European "norm", underlines the critical potential of integrating non-essentialist historical perspectives in research on EU and international politics. Moreover, such findings should caution against assuming that words have an inherent meaning and sharpen our attention towards striving to account for transformations in the constitution of discursive objects, mechanisms of exclusion and discursive "invasions, struggles, plundering, disguises, ploys" (Foucault 1977: 139). The specificity and borders that were identified in contemporary textual regularities, such as the exclusion of "populist" or "extremist" positions, the equation between democracy, representation, elections and party pluralism, or the understanding of "democracy" as a principle or name relevant to the analysis of the political system, all "pose the question of power" (Foucault 1972: 120). That is, if we accept the assumption that discourse is productive rather than a mere reflection of material reality and that the social sciences are a salient sight in producing authoritative knowledge about society, politics, democracy and so forth, it follows that there are no innocent definitions of "democracy" and that neutral, objective investigations of "democratic" norm diffusion, compliance or causal conditions for the success of democratic "norm export" strictly speaking are not possible. By means of illustration, the question whether democracy is applicable to the "economy" or confined to the "political" realm, and the related issue of how the border between such dichotomous comprehensive systems is drawn, is intimately connected with power and exclusion as it determines whether or not speaking about democracy in the economic realm makes sense. That is, for instance, whether or not the normative connotation of the term "democracy" could be seen to support calls for equality in wealth and distribution. To provide another example, a discursive regularity locating democracy in close proximity to terms such as "stability" and "trust" in leaders or established institutions lends itself to the exclusion of antagonist positions and critiques of political-economic elites.

Against such a backdrop, the findings can be seen to translate into a critique of objectivist, positivist epistemologies, but can also be taken as an impetus for joining recent calls by a number of IR scholars for studying discursive contestation and (re)production in international governance (Deitelhoff 2009, 2012; Wiener 2007; Vetterlein et al 2013). The empirical illustration of historical contingency might serve to caution against the reifying effects of objectivist epistemologies, regardless of their position on the rationalist – (ontological, "moderate") constructivist scale often applied in IR, while pointing to the relevance of further studies adopting a self-reflexive position by looking at knowledge within the social sciences themselves and investigating further aspects of the ordering, productive effects of scientific discourse. I therefore see great potential in future empirical analyses focusing on academic text and speech, while seeking to integrate discourse analysis and IR with STS and/or ANT on a theoretical level.

Finally, the present investigation also illustrated some of the limitations inherent to the methodology it sought to apply, with nuances and internal differences between authors and positions being blackened out to the benefit of mapping the outer borders of textuality (cf. for instance 3.4). While applying an archeological approach to contemporary text material proved to be useful in identifying mechanisms of exclusion, in grasping the borders of objects and the specificity of discursive connections between them, the genealogical consideration of historical material was well suited to illustrate the contingency of the latter. For future research, however, a more extensive genealogy of "democracy" encompassing text material from further points in the thread of discourse connecting 19th-century liberal thought with present orders of speech would be an additional interesting path.

Bibliography

Adler, Emanuel (1992): The Emergence of Cooperation: National Epistemic Communities and the International Evolution of the Idea of Nuclear Arms Control. In: *International Organization,* 46 (1), 101-145.

Adler, Emanuel / Haas, Peter M. (1992). Conclusion: Epistemic Communities, World Order, and the Creation of a Reflective Research Program. In: *International Organization,* 46 (1), 367-390.

Adler, Emanuel / Pouliot, Vincent (2011): International Practices. In: *International Theory* 3: 1–36.

Anderson, Stephanie/Seitz, Thomas R. (2006): European Security and Defence Policy Demystified: Nation-Building and Identity in the European Union. In: *Armed Forces and Society* 33 (24), 24-42.

Ashley, Richard / Walker, Rob B.J (1990): Reading Dissidence/Writing the Discipline: Crisis and the Question of Sovereignty in International Studies. In: International Studies Quarterly, (34), 367–416.

Barany, Zoltan/Moser, Robert G. (2009): *Is Democracy Exportable?* Cambridge: Cambridge University Press.

Burnell, Peter (2000): *Democracy Assistance: International Co-operation for Democratization.* London: Franck Cass.

- (2007): *Does international democracy promotion work?* Bonn: Deutsches Institut für Entwicklungspolitik. Discussion Paper (17).

Burron, Neil (2011): Unpacking U.S. Democracy Promotion in Bolivia From Soft Tactics to Regime Change. In: *Latin American Perspectives*, 39 (1), 115-132.

- (2012): Curbing 'Anti-Systemic' Tendencies in Peru: democracy promotion and the US contribution to producing neoliberal hegemony. In: *Third World Quarterly* 32 (9), 1655– 1672.

Buzan, Barry / Wæver, Ole / de Wilde, Jaap (1998): *Security: A New Framework for Analysis.* Boulder CO: Lynne Reinner.

Börzel, Tanja/Risse, Thomas (2004): *One Size Fits All! EU Policies for the Promotion of Human Rights, Democracy and the Rule of Law.* Prepared for the Worksho on Democracy Promotion, Oct. 4-5, 2004, Center for Development, Democracy, and the Rule of Law, Stanford University.

Börzel, Tanja/Risse, Thomas (2009): Venus approaching Mars? The European Union as an Emerging Civilian World Power. *Berliner Arbeitspapier zur Europäischen Integration* (11).

Carter, RGS (2006): Of Things Said and Unsaid: Power, Archivial Silence and Power in Silence. In: *Archivaria (61): Special Section on Archives, Space and Po*wer. http://journals.sfu.ca/archivar/index.php/ archivaria/article/viewFile/12541/13687 (10.08.2014)

Collins, Harry M./ Pinch, Trevor (1998): *The Golem: What You Should Know about Science.* New York: Cambridge University Press.

Cox, Michael/Ikenberry, John/Inoguchi, Takashi (2000): *American Democracy Promotion : Impulses, Strategies, and Impacts.* Oxford: Oxford University Press.

Campbell, David (1992): *Writing security: United States foreign policy and the politics of identity.* Glasgow: University of Minnesota Press.

- (2007): Poststructuralism. Dunne, Timl/Kurki, Milja/Smith, Steve: International Relations Theories. Oxford: Oxford University Press, 203-228.

Craner, Lorne W./Wollack, Kenneth (2008): *New Directions for Democracy Promotion.* Washington, D.C.: Better World Campaign, International Republican Institute & National Democractic Institute.

Cross, Mai'a K. Davis (2013): Rethinking Epistemic Communities Twenty Years Later. In: *Review of International Studies*, 39 (1), 137-160.

Deitelhoff, Nicole (2009): The Discursive Process of Legalization. Charting Islands of Persuasion in the ICC case. In: *International Organization,* 63 (1), 33-66.

Der Derian, James /Shapiro, Micheal (1989): *International/Intertextual Relations*. Lexington Mass.: Lexington Publishers.

Diamond, Larry (2008): *The Spirit of Democracy.* New York: Times Books.

Diaz-Bone, Rainer (1999): Probleme und Strategien der Operationalisierung des Diskursmodells im Anschluß an Michel Foucault. In: Bublitz, Hanelore u.a. (Hrsg.): *Das Wuchern der Diskurse*. Frankfurt am Main: Campus Verlag, 119-135.

Diez, Thomas (1999) *Die EU lesen: Diskursive Knotenpunkte in der britischen Europadebatte*. Opladen: Leske und Budrich.

- (2005): Constructing the Self and Changing Others: Reconsidering `Normative Power Europe. In: *Millennium - Journal of International Studies*, 33 (3), 613-636.

- (2007): Postmoderne Ansätze. In: Schieder, Siegfried/Spindler, Manuela (eds.): *Theorien der Internationalen Beziehungen.* Opladen: Budrich, 471-498.

Diez, Thomas / Manners, Ian (2007): Reflecting on Normative Power Europe. In: Berenskoetter, Felix/ Williams, M. J. (eds.): *Power in World Politics.* New York: Routledge, 173-188.

European Commission (2011a): The EU Neighbourhood. Joint Communication to the European Council, the European Parliament, the Council, the European Economic and Social Committee and the Committee of the Regions. A Partnership for Democracy and Shared Prosperity with the Southern Mediterranean. Brussels, 8 March 2011, COM(2011) 200 final.

- (2011b): A New Response to a Changing Neighbourhood. A review of European Neighbourhood Policy. Joint Communication to the European Parliament, the Council, the European Economic and Social Committee and the Committee of the Regions. Brussels, 25 May 2011, COM(2011) 303.

European Endowment for Democracy (2014): *Our Mission.* Available online: https://democracyendowment.eu (22.02.2014)

Fairclough, Norman ed. (2013): Language, Ideology, Power. In: Fairclough, Norman ed.: *Critical discourse analysis: The critical study of language*. Routledge, 25-84.

Fishkin, James / Laslett, Peter eds. (2003). *Debating Deliberative Democracy*. Wiley-Blackwell.

Foucault, Michael [1970] 2010: The Discourse on Language. In: *Archeology of Knowledge.* New York: Vintage, 215-37. - [1969] (2002): *The*

Archeology of Knowledge. London and New York: Routledge.

- (1977). Nietzsche, Genealogy, History. In: Bouchard, D. F. (ed.): *Language, Counter- Memory, Practice: Selected Essays and Interviews*. Ithaca: Cornell University Press.

- [1979] (2008): *The Birth of Biopolitics: Lectures at the Collège de France 1978–1979*. Basingstoke: Palgrave Macmillan.

- (1984): *What is Enlightenment?* http://sites.sdjzu.edu.cn/zhangpeizhong /what%20si %20enlightenment.pdf (13.10.2014)

Grevi/Helly/Keohane eds. (2009): *European Security and Defence Policy. The First Ten Years (1999-2009)*. Paris: EUISS.

Guilhot, Nicolas (2005): *The Democracy Makers: Human Rights and International Order*. New York: Columbia University Press.

Hamilton, Andrew (2009): J.S. Mill's Elitism: A Classical Liberal's Response to the Rise of Democracy. In: Kofmel, E. (ed): *Anti-Democratic Thought*. Exeter: Imprint Academic, 49- 66.

Hansen, Lene (2006): *Security as Practice. Discourse Analysis and the Bosnian War*. Oxon/New York: Routledge.

Hobson, Christopher (2009): Beyond the End of History: The Need for a 'Radical Historicisation' of Democracy in International Relations. In: *Millennium: Journal of International Studies*, 37 (3), 631-657.

Holzscheiter, Anna (2010): *Children's Rights in International Politics: The Transformative Power of Discourse*. Houndmills, Basingstoke: Palgrave Macmillian.

- (2011): Power of discourse or discourse of the powerful? The reconstruction of global childhood norms in the drafting of the UN Convention on the Rights of the Child. In: *Journal of Language and Politics*, 10(1), 1-28.

- (2013): Between Communicative Interaction and Structures of Signification: Discourse Theory and Analysis in IR. In: *International Studies Perspectives*, 1-21.

Jäger, Siegfried (2001): Diskurs und Wissen. In: Keller, Rainer et al (eds.): *Handbuch Sozialwissenschaftlicher Diskursanalyse*. Opladen:

Leske und Bundrich, 81-112.

Keller, Reiner (2005). Analysing Discourse. An Approach From the Sociology of Knowledge [33 paragraphs]. *Forum Qualitative Sozialforschung / Forum: Qualitative Social Research*, 6(3), Art. 32, http://nbn-resolving.de/urn:nbn:de:0114-fqs0503327 (30.05.2014)

Kennedy, Ryan (2013): The role of supranational identity in promoting democratic values. In: *European Union Politics*, 14(2), 228-249.

Kerchner, Brigitte (2006a): „Endlich Ordnung in der Werkzeugkiste". Zum Potential der Foucaultschen Diskursanalyse für die Politikwissenschaft In: Kerchner, Brigitte /Schneider, Silke (Hrsg.): *Foucault: Diskursanalyse der Politik. Eine Einführung*. Wiesbaden: VS Verlag für Sozialwissenschaften, 9-30.

- (2006b): Diskursanalyse in der Politikwissenschaft. Ein Forschungsüberblick. In: Kerchner, Brigitte /Schneider, Silke (Hrsg.): *Foucault: Diskursanalyse der Politik. Eine Einführung*. Wiesbaden: VS Verlag für Sozialwissenschaften, 33-67.

- (2006c): Wirklich Gegendenken. Politik analysieren mit Michel Foucault. In: Kerchner, Brigitte /Schneider, Silke (Hrsg.): *Foucault: Diskursanalyse der Politik. Eine Einführung*. Wiesbaden: VS Verlag für Sozialwissenschaften, 145-164.

- (2011): Diskursanalyse der Intersektionalität, in: Vinz, Dagmar/ Smykalla, Sandra (Hrsg.): *Intersektionalität – Theorien, Methoden und Politiken der Chancengleichheit.* Münster: Westphälisches Dampfboot, 140-157.

Kurki, Milja (2010): Democracy and Conceptual Contestability: reconsidering conceptions of democracy in democracy promotion. In: *International Studies Review*, 12(3), 362 - 86.

Laclau, Ernesto / Mouffe, Chantal (1990): *Hegemonie und radikale Demokratie: Zur Dekonstruktion des Marxismus.* Wien.

Lavenex, Sandra/Schimmelfennig, Frank (2009): EU rules beyond EU borders: theorizing external governance in European politics. In: *Journal of European Public Policy*, 16(6), 791–812.

- (2011): EU democracy promotion in the neighbourhood: from leverage to governance? In: *Journal of European Public Policy*, 18(4), 885-909.

Law, John / Hassard, John eds. (1999): *Actor Network Theory and After.* Oxford: Blackwell.

Lefort, Claude [1981] (2006): The Permanence of the Theological-Political. In: Hent de Vries (ed.): *Political Theologies: Public Religions in a Post-Secular World.* Fordham University Press, 153-159.

- (1990): Die Frage der Demokratie. In: Rödel, Ulrich (Hg.): *Autonome Gesellschaft und libertäre Demokratie*. Frankfurt am Main: Suhrkamp, 281- 297.

- [1969] (2008): Die neue Unordnung. In: Ders.: *Die Bresche*: Essays zum Mai 68. Wien: Turia + Kant.

Manners, Ian (2002): Normative Power Europe: A Contradiction in Terms? In: *Journal of Common Market Studies*, 40 (2), 235-58.

Marchart, Oliver (2007): Eine demokratische Gegenhegemonie. Zur neogramscianischen Demokratietheorie bei Laclau und Mouffe. In: Fischer-Lescano, Andreas / Buckel, Sonja (Hg.): *Hegemonie gepanzert mit Zwang. Zivilgesellschaft und Politik im Staatsverständnis von Antonio Gramsci,* Baden-Baden: Nomos, S.105-120.

Mouffe, Chantal (2000): *The Democratic Paradox*. London: Verson Books. - (2007): *Über das Politische - Wider die kosmopolitische Illusion*. Frankfurt am Main.

Müller, Harald (2004): Arguing, Bargaining and All That: Communicative Action, Rationalist Theory and the Logic of Appropriateness in International Relations. In: *European Journal of International Relations,* (10), 395–435.

Onuf, Nicholas (2013): *World of Our Making: Rules and Rule in Social Theory and International Relations*. Oxon: Routledge.

Piccone, Ted/Youngs, Richard (2006): *Strategies for Democratic Change.* Washington D.C., Democracy Coalition Project.

Rancière, Jacques [1969] (1979): Zur Theorie der Ideologie. Die Politik Althussers. In: Rancière, Jacques: *Wider den akademischen Marxismus.* Berlin, 5-50.

- (2002): *Das Unvernehmen.* Suhrkamp Verlag: Frankfurt am Main.

- (2005) : *La haine de la démocratie*. Floch, Mayenne : La fabrique éditions.

Risse, Thomas (2000) Let's Argue! Communicative Action in World Politics. In: *International Organization*, (54), 1–39.

Robinson, William I. (1996): *Promoting Polyarchy: Globalization, US Intervention, and Hegemony.* Cambridge: Cambridge University Press.

- (2013): Promoting Polyarchy: 20 years later. In: *International Relations* 27(2), 228-234.

Rogers, James (2007): From 'Civilian Power' to 'Global Power': Explicating the European Union's 'Grand Strategy' Through the Articulation of Discourse Theory. In: *Journal of Common Market Studies 47 (4)*, 831-62.

Rowland, Nicolas / Passoth, Jan-Hendrik / Kinney, Alexis (2011): REVIEW: Latour, Reassembling the Social. In: *Spontaneous Generations,* 5(1), 95-99.

Saar, Martin (2008): Understanding Genealogy: History, Power, and the Self. In: *Journal of the Philosophy of History,* (2), 295-314.

Schimmelfennig, Frank/Scholtz, Hanno (2008): EU Democracy Promotion in the European Neighbourhood. In: *European Union Politics* (9), 187- 215.

Simmons, P. (2011): The State of the Art in the EU Democracy Promotion Literature. In: *Journal of Contemporary European Research,*7(1), 129-142.

Sismondo, S. (2009): *An Introduction to Science and Technology Studies.* 2nd ed. Wiley-Blackwell.

Stielike (2009): *Wie regieren in Afrika? Eine genealogische Aussagenanalyse in governementalitättheoretischer Perspektive*. Freie Universität Berlin: Diplomarbeit.

Thompson, Dennis (2008). Deliberative Democratic Theory and Empirical Political Science. In: *Annual Review of Political Science,* (11), 497-520.

van Rompuy, Herman/ Barroso, José Manuel (2012): Joint statement on the award of the 2012 Nobel Peace Prize to the European Union, Brussels, 12 October 2012, EUCO 186/12.

Vetterlein, Antje / Wiener, Antje (2013): Gemeinschaft Revisited: Die sozialen Grundlagen internationaler Ordnung. In: *Ordnung und Wandel in der Weltpolitik Konturen einer Soziologie der Internationalen Beziehungen, Leviathan*, Special Issue 28.

Wæver, Ole (1995). Securitization and desecuritization. In: Lipschutz (ed.): *On security*. NY: Columbia University Press, 46-86.

Wolff, Jonas (2013): *After Hegemony: Normative contestation of democracy promotion in a pluralist world.* Paper presented at the 8th Pan-European Conference on International Relations,18– 21 September, Warsaw, Poland.

Youngs, Richard (2002): *The European Union and the Promotion of Democracy.* United States: Oxford University Press.

- (2008): Trends in Democracy Assistance: What has Europe Been Doing? In: *Journal of Democracy* 19(2), 160-9.

- (2009: Democracy Promotion as External Governance. In: *Journal of European Public Policy,* 16 (6), 895-915.

Primary Text Material

1st Text Corpus: JCMS

JCMS: *Journal of Common Market Studies*, 2004 – 2014, Issues 42(1) – 52(4)*

* In-depth analysis of all articles and reviews containing the word "democracy" (134 articles, approximately 50 reviews). All issues are available and searchable online:

http://onlinelibrary.wiley.com/journal/10.1111/%28ISSN%291468-5965 (05.07.2014)

2nd Text Corpus: 19th Century Liberalism

Mill, John Stuart [1861] (2001): *Considerations on Representative Government.* Ontario: Batoche Books.

- [1859] (2001): *On Liberty.* Ontario: Batoche Books.

Constant, Benjamin [1819]: *The Liberty of the Ancients compared to that of the Moderns.* http://www.uark.edu/depts/comminfo/cambridge/ ancients.html (04.08.2014)

de Tocqueville, Alexis [1835] (2003): *On Democracy in America.* Electronic Classics Series Publication: Pennsylvania State University.